Politics in Minnesota

POLITICS IN MINNESOTA

G. Theodore Mitau

CHAIRMAN, DEPARTMENT OF POLITICAL SCIENCE
MACALESTER COLLEGE

University of Minnesota Press, **MINNEAPOLIS**

Printed in the United States of America at the
Jones Press, Inc., Minneapolis

3 2

Library of Congress Catalog Card Number: 60-10880

PUBLISHED IN GREAT BRITAIN, INDIA, AND PAKISTAN BY THE
OXFORD UNIVERSITY PRESS, LONDON, BOMBAY, AND KARACHI
AND IN CANADA BY THOMAS ALLEN, LTD., TORONTO

Second Printing 1960

*The author wishes to express his appreciation for the encourage-
ment and support given him by the Minnesota Citizenship Clearing
House and the National Citizenship Clearing House in
preparation of this study.*

FOREWORD

THERE must be many citizens of Minnesota and many political observers elsewhere who have long felt the need for just such a book as this — a brief, systematic, reliable, and up-to-date account of politics in Minnesota. It provides information and insights to be found in no other book now available. Recent and contemporary political leaders like John A. Johnson, Theodore Christianson, Floyd B. Olson, Harold E. Stassen, Luther W. Youngdahl, Hubert H. Humphrey, and Orville L. Freeman march by in brief review, while the Republican and Democratic parties, the Nonpartisan League, the Democratic-Farmer-Labor party, and minor political groups and movements (even to the Communists), with their varied ups and downs and transformations, make up an ever-living, ever-changing background. There are substantial and informative chapters on current political problems, also — on the state's election laws and party organizations, on the "nonpartisan partisan legislature," and on lobbying before the legislature. The supplementary materials at the end of the volume contain in easy reference form highly interesting and useful information, both biographical and statistical.

The author has qualified himself for the writing of this book by long study and the preparation of special articles in the field. He has in fact made himself an important authority on Minnesota politics. His style is necessarily compact, to say so much in so little space, but at the same time it is clear, flexible, and interesting.

It is my hope that this book will have a wide reading. No one can understand the government and politics of the United States as a whole, or be an effective citizen in national, state, or local affairs, without knowing a great deal about politics in his own and other states.

Let us hope that this book will be followed by another in which the actual organization and workings of state and local government in Minnesota are set forth, and the great issues of public policy are discussed. I refer, of course, to state and local administrative organization, the judicial system, the state and local services, budgeting and finance, the interrelations of state and local governments, and the operation of the process of popular government as a whole. These call for another book.

In the meantime, we owe thanks to the author of this one for a fine start along the road to greater political understanding.

WILLIAM ANDERSON
University of Minnesota

February 1960

CONTENTS

Politics in Minnesota

1

PARTY PATTERNS, ISSUES, AND LEADERS

CONSERVATIVE in its governmental institutions, often liberal and sometimes radical in its politics, Minnesota offers a fascinating study in contrasts.

The state's constitution is one of the oldest in the nation: in fundamental principle and framework it is today the same charter that was ratified by Congress in 1858 when Minnesota entered the Union as the thirty-second state. It has been amended 85 times — but almost two-thirds of all constitutional changes submitted to the voters since 1900 have been rejected, and periodic proposals for a thoroughgoing revision through a new constitutional convention have been unsuccessful.

The government of the state has the traditional division of powers among executive, judicial, and legislative branches. (Its one unusual aspect is the officially "nonpartisan" character of the legislature — since 1913 state senators and representatives have been elected on a ballot that does not identify candidates by party label.) Only slowly has the machinery of state government been modified to accommodate changes in the lives of its citizens as Minnesota developed from the near-frontier, largely rural economy of the late 1850's, when the population was 150,000, to the complex modern society and more than 3 million population at the end of the 1950's. The regular term of the legislature, for example, was in 1959 still that established in 1887 — 90 days every two years — although legislative business had increased severalfold in the interim. And the districts in which legislators run for office were the same in the 1958 election as in 1912, despite large shifts in population from district to district over the years. To some degree change has been accomplished in all three branches, but the pace has been deliberate.

Yet, while reluctant to make innovations in the state's basic governmental structure, Minnesotans have not hesitated to experiment politically whenever their needs were not being met. When farm prices dropped, when credit was tight, when thousands were unemployed, the state's discontented swelled the ranks of third parties that challenged the power of corporate wealth, privilege, and monopoly, and demanded public ownership or control of warehouses, utilities, and railroads. Immigrants and natives, prohibitionists and suffragettes, farmers and laborers, in ever-changing coalitions of principle or convenience, attacked social and economic problems. Sometimes they worked through third or minor parties, sometimes they struggled within the primaries of the major parties; but whatever their methods, they fought with righteous zeal for their conceptions of social justice and good government.

In the dynamics of Minnesota politics, party lines have never seemed sacred. Significant numbers of voters show no hesitancy in crossing over, splitting their ticket, supporting "the man rather than the party." In 1956 a majority of Minnesotans voted for the Republican presidential candidate, Eisenhower, while electing a Democratic governor, Freeman. Similarly in 1904 and 1908 the election results paired a Republican president (Theodore Roosevelt and Taft) and a Democratic governor (Johnson). In the national elections of the 1940's Democrats Franklin D. Roosevelt and Truman won the state's presidential electors, but Republicans Stassen, Thye, and Youngdahl captured the governorship. The independent spirit of the Minnesota voter is a significant political fact of life in the state. It may be traced in part to the third-party tradition and in part to the tradition of nonpartisan elections of local officials as well as state legislators, both of which have increased the fluidity of party alignments.

At the same time there has been no absence of intense partisanship in Minnesota — lively, raucous, bitter party battles have

4

colored the state's history down to the present, when two strong major parties contend for votes — and power — in campaigns less physically violent perhaps than some of the past, but no less verbally vigorous. And the political leaders who have put their mark on the state, and have claimed national attention as well, have been closely associated with party movements. A prominent Democratic presidential candidate in 1960, Senator Hubert H. Humphrey is the latest in this line of imaginative, and controversial, men, which includes Ignatius Donnelly, sometime Republican, Anti-Monopolist, Greenbacker, Populist; Democrat John A. Johnson; Farmer-Laborite Floyd B. Olson; and Republicans Harold E. Stassen and Luther W. Youngdahl. They and the several parties whose fortunes they shared and influenced have contributed richly to the shaping of the present political character of the state.

It is appropriate, then, to begin this brief introduction to politics in Minnesota by tracing certain of the party patterns in the first century of its statehood. A comprehensive political history cannot be attempted here. But it is hoped that the sketch that follows, incomplete though it is, will set the scene, so to speak, for the discussion of special characteristics of contemporary Minnesota politics in later chapters. Some of the names and dates and statistics that must be omitted in the narrative will be found in the supplementary materials at the end of this book.

Republican hegemony, 1858–1904

The state of Minnesota was born in an era of high partisan feelings. Even during the territorial period questions concerning the extension of slavery, prohibition of liquor traffic, railroad and land speculation, and voting rights for immigrants divided Democrats from newly created Republicans and sparked impressive displays of fervor and invective.

But the most dramatic demonstration of party hostility came in the state constitutional convention of 1857. With a frontier society's disregard for procedural niceties, it had been called by a special session of the territorial legislature which did not have a right to call it, and upon the signature of a governor who had no right to so act while outside the territorial limits; it was attended by more delegates than were entitled to accreditation; and it permitted participation by some whose certificates were issued in clear violation of the letter and spirit of the election laws. Nearly six weeks were required to organize the convention, and even then, the delegates refused to assemble in the same room; they never deliberated as one body and never affixed their signatures to a single document. Minnesota still preserves two basic charters, one drafted and signed by the Democratic wing of the convention, the other by the Republican wing. Both are official. Though they are substantially alike, there are more than three hundred minor differences in punctuation and phraseology.

The first gubernatorial election was likewise the occasion of intense rivalry between the parties. After a bitter campaign, a Democrat, Henry H. Sibley, became the first governor of the state in 1858. But a Republican, Alexander Ramsey, replaced him in 1860, and for most of four decades thereafter the Republican party dominated Minnesota. From 1860 to 1904 only one non-Republican was elected to the governorship; the state legislature remained under Republican control except for the 1891 session; 36 of the 50 representatives in Congress from Minnesota during this period were Republicans. The state's voters consistently supported Republican presidential candidates by heavy majorities.

Republicanism did not rule unchallenged, however. This was a period of explosive growth in population, from 172,000 in 1860 to 1,751,000 in 1900, and of rapid social and economic change; when the party in power did not respond quickly enough in satisfying new needs and curbing new abuses, one or another of a succession of third parties appeared as the highly vocal champion of reform. The Democrats too, while relatively ineffective at the polls and badly torn by internal dissension, remained critics to be reckoned with. The political winds stirred up by rival parties were felt in Republican councils, and influenced to some extent Republican policy. At the state level, as at the national, a number of the specific reforms espoused by protest groups found their way into major party platforms, and finally into law.

In Minnesota agrarian discontent was the focus of third-party movements, as declining prices, discriminatory railroad practices, tight credit, and the currency shortage squeezed the once self-sufficient farmer. Wheat became king in the state, and farmers were ever-increasingly dependent for their livelihood upon the huge corporations that regulated the transportation and sale of their major crop. The platforms of the Anti-Monopolists, the Greenbackers, the Farmers' Alliance, and the Populists from the 1870's through the 1890's crystallized the grievances of the farmer. The railroads were condemned for their discriminatory practices, their unscrupulous collusion with warehouse and elevator interests, their watered stock; Minneapolis wheat combines were accused of ruthless speculation and monopolistic price-fixing. As early as 1873 the Anti-Monopolists and Greenbackers demanded state surveillance of corporations and railroads.

Minnesota third parties did not, however, limit their interests to the welfare of farmers only. In 1872 the Prohibition party called for the immediate enfranchisement of women. In 1879 the Greenbackers advocated a "graduated and equitable" income tax and an outright end to the employment of children under fourteen. In 1888 the Farm and Labor party demanded the Australian ballot, the eight-hour day, employer liability for workmen's injuries, and a sizable number of other reforms.

Implicit in the programs of all these groups was a new concept of government — the idea that the state should take unto itself greater responsibility for economic justice, exercising its latent powers to protect the public interest against private privilege.

One of the most colorful personalities associated with Minnesota third parties was Ignatius Donnelly. A man of wide-ranging literary and social as well as political interests, Donnelly has been called "the universal genius of the prairies." During his eventful career he was elected state lieutenant governor and representative to Congress under the Republican banner; he served in the state legislature as an independent; he was spokesman for one third-party movement as editor of the *Anti-Monopolist*; he was an unsuccessful candidate for governor on the Populist ticket in 1892; and at various times he held positions of importance with the several agrarian reform groups. His powers of oratory were considerable, and his energy boundless, but another Minnesota liberal, Sidney M. Owen, Farmers' Alliance candidate for governor in 1890 and editor of *Farm, Stock and Home*, was a steadier and perhaps a more influential leader in the state's protest politics.

Although Owen was defeated for governor the protest movement had a taste of victory in 1890, for the Farmers' Alliance and Democrats took advantage of a three-party deadlock to capture both houses of the legislature. But the Republicans regained control in 1892, and not until 1898 did the various protest groups cooperate effectively to elect a governor. In that year, John Lind, supported by Democrats, Populists, and Silver Republicans, was swept into office.

But radical reform was not in the offing. Lind himself was by no means a rabid reformer, and he was powerless to carry even his moderate program against a solid Republican front in the legislature. He served only one term, and Republican governors were elected in 1900 and 1902.

In 1904, however, the Republican dynasty was broken, by the 43-year-old editor of the *St. Peter Herald*, John A. Johnson.

A Democratic interlude, 1904–1910

In a Horatio Alger era Johnson was an embodiment of the "rags to success" tradition. He was born on a farm near St. Peter, into a Swedish immigrant family less than ten years in their new country. His blacksmith father succumbed to alcoholism, deserted the family, and died later in a poorhouse, leaving Mrs. Johnson to take in washing and her 13-year-old son to begin a career that was finally to put him in the governor's chair for three terms and bring nomination for the presidency within view.

Successful as a journalist (he was elected president of the Minnesota Editorial Association at the age of 32), Johnson was at first unsuccessful in his bid for the state legislature, but in 1898 he was elected to the state senate. His vigorous campaigning and political acumen in the legislature caught the attention of the state Democratic leaders, and he became their gubernatorial candidate in 1904.

These were days before the automobile, radio, and television brought candidates ubiquitously to the electorate, but in a month and a half Johnson barnstormed through 74 of Minnesota's then 84 counties to deliver a total of 102 speeches. Republican strength, already sapped by internal feuds, wilted before such a barrage, and Johnson defeated his Republican opponent by 7,000 votes — this while Theodore Roosevelt was carrying the state 216,000 to 55,000 over Alton B. Parker. He was re-elected in 1906 by a 74,000 majority, and his popularity remained strong in 1908.

Johnson was a "reform" governor, who drew on Populist and other Progressive support. He was devoted to conservation, to curtailment of railroad abuses, to protecting the public weal against utility privileges; he never hesitated to defend the downtrodden. But he never lost his sense of proportion; he was never a demagogue.

The legislature remained under Republican control during Johnson's tenure in office. But he secured bipartisan backing for a number of significant measures. Codes were enacted regulating insurance companies and timber sales on state lands. Inheritance laws were tightened. Railroads were prohibited from issuing free passes to officeholders, thus ending an abuse long decried by reform groups because it opened the door to "undue influence," if not to outright peculation by public officials who rode free but collected travel allowances from the public treasury. Another long-time plank of third-party platforms became law when cities were empowered to own and operate public utilities.

Johnson's achievements were bringing him a national reputation, enhanced by speaking engagements throughout the country. To Democrats who found William Jennings Bryan too radical for comfort, Johnson seemed an attractive alternative. A few Johnson-for-President clubs sprang up around the country in 1908, but Bryan had a long head start, and the Democratic National Convention gave him 888½ votes to Johnson's 46. The Minnesota governor was still very young for a presidential candidate, however, only 47, and his supporters looked forward eagerly to 1912.

Then, in 1909, following abdominal surgery, Johnson died. Ordinarily non-demonstrative Minnesotans "wept in the streets," and some fifty thousand people viewed his body as it lay in state. He had been the "people's governor," as his biographer calls him, and their sense of loss at his death was deep and personal. His death also ended the first sustained Democratic leadership in the state, for during two decades after 1910 (with the exception of one two-year term), Republicans again dominated the governorship.

Republican progressivism and farmer-labor protest, 1910–1930

Minnesota Republicanism during the 1910's and 1920's was strongly tinged with Roosevelt progressivism. Theodore Roosevelt carried the state in 1912 against Woodrow Wilson and William Howard Taft, and he long remained a popular symbol for liberal Republicans and for third-party mavericks, who found themselves much in sympathy with the governmental reforms he advocated: direct primaries, conservation of resources, curbing of trusts and special interests, for example.

During the Republican administrations of these years in Minnesota, legislative beginnings were made in such fields as cooperative marketing, regulation of grain-grading and cold-storage plants, workmen's compensation, aid to veterans in the form of bonus or tuition. A statewide primary law was adopted. Elections to the legislature were put on a nonpartisan basis. The highway system was expanded. A state industrial commission was created, as well as a rural credit system empowered to invest state funds in farm mortgages. Especially during the three terms of Theodore Christianson (1925–31), the administrative system of the state was reconstructed.

It was the Nonpartisan League that disturbed Republican calm in this period.

The League had been formed in 1915 by a group of North Dakota farmers under the inspired leadership of A. C. Townley. Its primary purpose was to secure public ownership of certain essential farm services and facilities — terminal elevators, flour mills, packing houses, and so on — so that farmers would not be at the mercy of irresponsible private enterprise. "Nonpartisan" in principle, the League was not conceived as a separate political party but was to work for the candidates of its choice through the primaries and conventions of the established parties.

Likened by one historian to a prairie fire, the League swept swiftly over North Dakota and spread to Minnesota, where its program made sense to Red River Valley and western Minnesota wheat farmers long resentful of middlemen, of the railroads, and of the Minneapolis grain exchange. The spirit of Populism was still very much alive among Minnesota farmers, and it responded quickly to the ingenious tactics of the League organizers. There was nothing subtle about the way Townley and his lieutenants descended on Minnesota in 1917. Specially trained organizers came in caravans of 80 or 90 cars and went to work systematically canvassing rural areas under the direction of small committees of local farmers.

Dedicated adherents multiplied — but so did opponents. And the League was vulnerable to attack in the war years of 1917 and 1918, because of the heavy German cast of its membership and because of the antiwar stand taken by a number of its leaders before the United States entered World War I. The Minnesota Public Safety Commission, directed by Governor Joseph A. A. Burnquist and Judge John F. McGee, was established to scrutinize groups suspected of being disloyal, and the League came under its severe condemnation. "A Nonpartisan League lecturer," said Judge McGee, "is a traitor every time. In other words, no matter what he says or does, a League worker is a traitor."

Townley and one of his aides were arrested, charged with antiwar conduct; injunctions against League meetings were issued

11

in nineteen counties; mob violence erupted here and there. Even so, the embattled Nonpartisan candidate for governor in the Republican primary of 1918, former Congressman Charles A. Lindbergh, although defeated, received 150,000 votes, a remarkable show of strength.

The League had early recognized that in Minnesota farm support would not be enough to win elections: the state's urban vote, much larger than in North Dakota, must also be tapped. Relations were established with labor groups as early as 1917, and in 1920 the League and the Working People's Nonpartisan Political League, made up of union members, supported a joint slate of candidates for state office, which was defeated. In 1922, after an attempt to fuse with the Democrats had failed, League adherents campaigned independently as the Farmer-Labor party; their candidate for governor, Magnus Johnson, came within 14,000 votes of winning and Farmer-Laborites did capture three congressional seats, two in the House and one in the Senate. The following year the Farmer-Labor group won the state's second Senate seat in a special election after the death of the incumbent.

But even this modest success was short-lived. It had been due in part to a sharp decline in farm prices, and with a general economic upswing in the middle twenties, and an accompanying conservative reaction, the new party's fortunes faltered. They were further undermined by the tactics of the American Communist party in the campaign preceding the national election of 1924. The Communist attempts to infiltrate the national third party that was supporting Robert M. LaFollette for president — with which the Minnesota Farmer-Labor group had strong ties — were widely publicized. LaFollette himself denounced the Communists, and the Farmer-Labor gubernatorial candidate, Floyd B. Olson, while failing to take the matter seriously enough to make a strong stand, denied Communist leanings. Public confidence was shaken, however, and the Communist issue contributed to the decisive defeat of state and national reform-party candidates.

Through the rest of the twenties, continued prosperity and the respected leadership of Governor Christianson kept the capitol in St. Paul a Republican stronghold.

The Farmer-Labor party in office, 1931–1939

With the Great Depression, what had been a radical element in the political ideology of the minority — governmental responsibility for the economic and social welfare of all citizens — became an imperative majority demand. The clamor for government action on behalf of the individual — the unemployed, the hungry, the distressed — united at least temporarily farmers and laborers, small business men, white-collar workers, and intellectuals. As the farm economy collapsed, businesses failed by the score, and industry slowed to snail's pace, Minnesotans, with the rest of the nation, looked for a political deliverer. In Floyd B. Olson they found a man whose temperament and abilities well suited the times — a rebel willing to try the unorthodox, a humanitarian deeply committed to the defense of the underprivileged, a leader of great personal magnetism who inspired devotion and confidence.

Like John A. Johnson, Olson came of Scandinavian immigrant stock. Like his predecessor too, Olson learned at first hand the problems of the "have nots." After a year at the University of Minnesota, he left his home on Minneapolis' north side to knock about the outside world as salesman, miner, and common laborer. His experience vastly broadened, he returned to Minneapolis, put himself through night law school, and embarked on a promising law practice. But his lifelong restlessness pushed him to livelier fields, and he sought and won the post of Hennepin County attorney.

Although he was a crusader against racketeering and city hall corruption, he showed genuine sympathy for petty criminals, whom he considered victims of an unjust social order rather than incorrigibles meriting severe punishment. He also championed organized labor against conservative business.

After his defeat in the 1924 gubernatorial race, Olson restricted his activities to Minneapolis for a time, but he kept his political fences in good repair and slowly began to build a reservoir of personal support — among Democrats and some Republicans as well as the stalwarts of the young Farmer-Labor party. He was ready when his opportunity came in 1930.

The campaign of that year was reminiscent of the crusades of Greenbackers, Progressives, and Nonpartisan Leaguers, as the young county attorney led the Farmer-Laborites to a resounding victory on a platform advocating many of the traditional third-party reforms, as well as immediate relief for the destitute. In winning the governorship, Olson carried 82 of the state's 87 counties. But his party captured only one of the state constitutional offices and only 29 state senatorships and 40 seats in the state house of representatives.

Despite the Farmer-Labor landslide, then, Olson did not enjoy a legislative majority during his first term, and his program had heavy going. But the 1932 election, which returned Olson to office with 50.6 per cent of the popular vote against 32.3 per cent for the Republicans and 16.4 per cent for the Democrats, also gave him substantial backing in the legislature. Important parts of his program were subsequently enacted into law: a mortgage moratorium bill was passed, protecting hard-pressed farmers against foreclosure; a state income tax was adopted; labor injunctions and "yellow dog" contracts were prohibited; a beginning was made in old-age pensions. However, the more extreme planks of the Farmer-Labor platform, such as public ownership of utilities and factories, unemployment and health insurance, outlawry of loan sharks, free distribution of school textbooks, and reduction of interest rates, were rejected.

During his three terms as governor, Olson was forced to weather one crisis after another: the deepening depression; the bloody Minneapolis truckers' strike of 1934; the Farm Holiday Association's march on the state capitol; bitter factional struggles for prestige and patronage within his own party, and embarrassing indiscretions of friends and appointees.

But Olson thrived on controversy. And his powerful personality and striking accomplishments in Minnesota were bringing him national prestige. In Washington, where he frequently represented the state, he was respected as one of the most effective of the nation's liberal governors. There was considerable support in 1936 for a national third-party ticket headed by Olson — support which he did little to encourage, for he was unwilling to hurt Franklin D. Roosevelt's chances in Minnesota.

At 45 Olson seemed promising presidential timber for the future. But, again, tragedy struck a favorite son of Minnesota. Late in the summer of 1936, on the eve of the election campaign in which he had hoped to run for the Senate, Floyd B. Olson died. The affection of the state's people for their fallen leader poured out in emotional torrents — as it had a generation or so earlier for Johnson. Friend and adversary alike joined in uncritical sorrow and praise.

In calmer perspective Olson may be seen as a figure of considerable stature in the protest-party tradition of the state, though by no means without failings, personal and political. A rebel at heart — "I am not a liberal," he once shouted; "I am what I want to be — I am a radical" — he was regarded by conservatives as little better than a card-carrying Communist. Yet his radicalism was perhaps pragmatic rather than theoretical; he saw welfare legislation on behalf of the farmer, the unemployed, and the aged in terms of simple social justice.

At any rate, wherever his sympathies tended, his political skill was such that during most of his administration he managed to keep in harness the more radical and the more conservative elements in the Farmer-Labor coalition.

Olson's fellow Farmer-Laborite Elmer Benson, who succeeded to the governorship in 1937, had no such skill. His difficulties were compounded by a resurgence of the Communist issue. Olson had likewise been plagued by Communist activities, but they came to a head during the Benson administration.

Challenges from the far left were not new in Minnesota. As we have seen, they harassed the Farmer-Labor movement of the twenties. Even earlier, various offshoots of European Marxism appeared in Minnesota. Numerically, these parties were never significant, rarely polling more than 1 per cent of the entire vote and at no time more than 10,000 for a state or federal office. Yet, since they campaigned vigorously and criticized the major parties relentlessly, they are of importance out of proportion to their size.

At the risk of greatly oversimplifying a complex matter, one might distinguish several major strains of American Marxism. First there were the "direct actionists" or revolutionary syndicalists. With the workers' syndicate or union as their social unit and with strikes, boycotts, and if necessary violence as their means, they aimed to exterminate capitalism and transform society, and to do all this without recourse to existing political methods and institutions. In Minnesota the group showing closest kinship to this tradition of irreconcilable class war was the Industrial Labor or Socialist Labor party (1900), which was affiliated with the national faction led by Daniel DeLeon. (The present Industrial Government party, which polled 5,785 votes in 1956, is often considered to be the ideologically orthodox but nonviolent and anti-Communist successor to the DeLeon tradition.)

Second, political socialism as practiced by several different groups reflected two opposed interpretations of Marxism, the one a moderate revisionism and the other a radical communism. Followers of the former theory insisted that socialism could be achieved through democratic means — by ballots rather than bullets; their aim was public ownership and/or control of basic industry. Candidates of their persuasion customarily used the Socialist or Public Ownership label when running for office. After Lenin founded the Third Internationale in 1919 and welded it into an instrument to direct radical Marxism in its worldwide battles, the more moderate socialists found themselves locked in acrimonious conflict with aggressive and totalitarian communism. Echoes of their internecine warfare were heard as far away as Minnesota's northern Finnish communities, where the so-called "Red" Finns disputed with the other Finnish socialist factions. Rallying around the perennial candidate Norman Thomas, the moderate socialists in Minnesota and elsewhere condemned Leninist-Stalinist terrorism as a gross perversion of Marxist theory; no less critical of Kremlinist communism were the Trotsky followers who appeared on Minnesota's presidential ballot as the Socialist Workers party in 1948.

Although as early as 1920 William Z. Foster, leader of the official American Communist party, the Kremlin-recognized affiliate of the Third Internationale, labeled the Farmer-Labor movement a party of the petty bourgeoisie, corrupt and opportunistic, a betrayer of the proletariat, his followers did not hesitate to attempt to infiltrate the group in 1924. In 1933 and 1934 the Communists exploited farmer-labor grievances and organized marches on the state capitol and mass demonstrations. Then, suddenly, a significant shift occurred in Communist world tactics. The new program of the Soviet Union (1935–36) was to create a grand alliance, a "popular front" of anti-Fascist and pro-democratic elements. In the United States, New Deal groups, the CIO, and many other organizations (including the Minnesota Farmer-Labor party) were to be cultivated and used as fronts for the new strategy. Leftist agitators were to play on Americans' sympathy for the Spanish Loyalists and horror at the growing Nazi menace. Though they were decent, sensitive, and fundamentally honest people, a few of the followers of the midwestern protest tradition fell victim to the Moscow line, which cleverly and callously used catchwords out of their own ideological heritage.

Governor Benson was deaf to critics in his own administration who warned him of the danger of betrayal of midwestern liberalism inherent in Communist tactics. Making little effort to conceal his annoyance, Benson labeled such admonitions the irresponsible smears of business interests seeking to cloud the true issues of unemployment and social injustice.

At the same time legislative investigations of irregularities in the state highway, conservation, and relief departments were providing additional political capital for critics.

The Farmer-Laborites were badly divided as the 1938 election approached. In a bitter campaign marked by extremes of vituperation, Hjalmar Petersen challenged incumbent Elmer Benson in the Farmer-Labor primary. Claiming to be the legitimate political heir of Olson, Petersen alleged that his opponent had "stolen" the party nomination in 1936 with the help of a "palace guard"; he accused the Benson administration of incompetence and indifference to Communist infiltration. This public washing of Farmer-Labor dirty linen was particularized by reporter Joseph H. Ball in the *St. Paul Dispatch-Pioneer Press*, from whence Republicans picked up details to good effect in fall campaigning. Though he survived the primary, Benson's vote-getting appeal had been irreparably damaged.

Farmer-Labor rule, then, was doomed and waiting only for the *coup de grâce*. This came at the hands of Harold E. Stassen, a young Dakota County attorney, who amassed in 1938 the largest majority ever received by a Minnesota governor up to that time.

Republican resurgence, 1939–1955

According to some sources, Stassen had felt political and even presidential aspirations as far back as his high school days. After a brilliant career at the University of Minnesota, where he took a law degree, he soon turned to active politics. Convinced of his own mission and persuaded of the haplessness of Republican leadership, he began during the depths of the Depression, in 1934, to make the party over by means of a Young Republican League. This movement attracted professional people, anti-leftist Progressives, young businessmen, reformers, and thousands more who could find political fellowship neither among the intransigent Republicans nor among the scandal-ridden Farmer-Laborites. While making a firm distinction between socialism and his own "enlightened capitalism," as he called it, Stassen was not blind to the usefulness of the milder New Deal proposals, as for example social legislation for the needy, the aged, and the dependent.

His 1938 campaign concentrated on a few essentials. In addition to capitalizing on the Communist issue, he advocated a civil service law to prevent in the future the patronage abuses which had discredited the Farmer-Laborites; new legislation to stabilize management-labor relations and prevent bloody strikes; administrative reorganization to save public money, increase efficiency, and preclude corruption and racketeering.

Farmer-Laborites scoffed at Stassen's claim to kinship with midwestern liberalism and progressivism. Was he not, they asked, the spokesman for United States Steel, meatpackers, and the utilities? The Republican old guard was hardly more enthusiastic about the "Boy Scout," as they termed him; they resented his youth (he was only 31 when elected) and his open cultivation of an "all-Stassen" organization. But he had an excellent press, largely due to the efforts of St. Paul reporter Joseph Ball, and he drew heavy support from customarily independent or nonpolitical segments of the electorate as well as from a hard core of young Republicans.

As the nation's youngest governor in 1939, Stassen achieved an impressive record. Under his leadership, the Minnesota legislature adopted a civil service system, increased social security benefits, extended the moratorium on mortgages, passed an anti-loan-shark bill. Stassen's reorganization of the state administration, his labor relations record, and his steady internationalism in the midst of pre-Pearl Harbor isolationism earned him widespread respect.

He was not without critics. His administration was accused of granting tax reductions to iron-ore companies, of permitting preferential tax valuations on utility company properties, and of inserting an old-age lien law into the old-age assistance program. Even more violently condemned was the "summer housecleaning" of 1939 which removed an unspecified number (the estimates range from 2,252 to 10,000) of Farmer-Labor appointees or sympathizers from public office just before the new civil service law went into effect.

On the whole, however, Stassen's program was highly regarded by Minnesota voters. A 1939 Gallup poll showed that 81 per cent of those queried approved his actions, and only 19 per cent disapproved. His large majorities in the 1940 and 1942 elections reaffirmed this popularity.

After 1939 foreign policy and the war loomed large in Minnesota politics. When isolationist Senator Ernest Lundeen died in 1940, Stassen appointed to complete the unexpired term his old friend and press advocate Joseph Ball, a confirmed internationalist like Stassen himself. Few appointments in the state's history caused more of a stir than this one. Although Ball had propelled the virtually unknown Stassen into prominence and had aided immeasurably his first campaign, Republican regulars were bitterly disappointed that Stassen had not rewarded a man of richer governmental experience and unquestioned party loyalty. But Stassen felt strongly that the troubled times required a man with the outlook of Ball. Both Stassen and Ball represented a break with the old midwestern tradition of isolationism which had been so powerfully articulated by Congressmen Charles A. Lindbergh, Harold Knutson, and Ernest Lundeen — all of whom had bitterly opposed United States entry into World War I.

In 1943 Stassen left Minnesota for service with the United States Navy, where his tour of duty as flag officer to Admiral W. F. Halsey enhanced his stature, as did his later participation in the United Nations charter conference in San Francisco.

After the war Stassen's presidential aspirations took him to greener fields for national politicking than Minnesota — whose relatively few electoral votes, eleven, and comparative lack of political prestige are significant disadvantages for ambitious politician-statesmen with an eye on the White House.

Stassen had his baptism in presidential politics in 1940, when he was floor manager for the successful nomination campaign of Wendell L. Willkie at the Republican National Convention. In 1948 he made his own serious bid for the nomination, but tactical miscalculations (contesting Taft delegates in the Ohio presidential preference primary, for example) caused rifts between him and the party regulars, and the convention gave its support to Thomas E. Dewey.

During the next four years as president of the University of Pennsylvania, he attempted to put down new political roots in the nationally influential keystone state, in preparation for the 1952 Republican convention. But this was to be the scene of deep disappointment to Stassen — and, ironically, it was developments in Minnesota that dealt the decisive blow to his hopes.

Stassen had led in the Minnesota Republican presidential primary, and most of the state's convention delegates were officially pledged to him. But a write-in campaign for Dwight D. Eisenhower, launched just a few days before the state primary, had resulted in what came to be called the "Minnesota miracle." With almost none of the advance publicity Stassen had enjoyed, and without the approval and aid of the national Eisenhower organization, the campaign was phenomenally successful: 108,692 voters took the trouble to write in Eisenhower's name on the ballot, while Stassen, whose name was printed thereon, received only some 20,000 more votes, 129,076. The majority of the Minnesota delegates to the convention took this as a popular mandate for the general turned college president, and before the first roll call had been officially closed the delegation switched its vote from Stassen to Eisenhower. Thus ended Stassen's second bid for the nomination.

Although appointed to high posts in the Eisenhower administration, Stassen was unsuccessful in two later bids for elective public office in Pennsylvania. A resourceful and creative leader, with a keen mind and boundless energy, he perhaps carries within him the tragic flaw of the traditional tragic protagonist; at any rate his critics view his overriding ambition for power as too ill concealed and as the primary cause of his reverses. Together with the apparent opportunism his critics point out and basic errors in political judgment, it has rendered him unable, at least so far, to recapture the place he had once held in the popular imagination as the boy wonder of Minnesota.

In 1943 Stassen had been succeeded in the Minnesota governorship by Lieutenant Governor Edward J. Thye, under whom the Stassen tradition was further developed. A major contribution of his administration was the establishment of the first Interracial Commission in the state. He remained in office until 1946, when he was elected to the United States Senate. Luther W. Youngdahl, who had served with distinction as a judge in district

court and state supreme court, continued the Republican gubernatorial line.

In his public pronouncements during his three terms as governor, Youngdahl, a devout Swedish Lutheran, proclaimed the
moral imperative of Christian participation in politics. Putting
into practice his own philosophy that "Christian conscience"
must be brought to bear on all phases of public as well as private
life, he directed the energies of his administration toward the
problems of youth, law enforcement, mental health, and human
relations. Significant legislation was accomplished. The youth
conservation act of 1947 provided for specialized rehabilitation
treatment for juvenile offenders; an anti-slot-machine act of 1947
was designed to curb all major forms of gambling; a comprehensive mental health act was adopted in 1949. By executive decree
Negroes were admitted into the National Guard on an integrated
basis. From the podium and the pulpit Youngdahl campaigned
throughout the state for these and other reforms which gained
enthusiastic support from socially conscious members of diver-
gent religious and political faiths; proposals for the granting of
the power of arrest to liquor control officers and for a statewide
Fair Employment Practices Commission are further examples.

The Republican party during the Youngdahl era was an interesting amalgam of old-guard stalwarts, former Stassenites, new-
comers attracted by the governor's reforms, and temporarily
Republican independents. When Youngdahl accepted a federal
district judgeship in the District of Columbia in July 1951, the
Minneapolis Star was moved to comment: "With Youngdahl
out of the picture, one observer has suggested [that] Republicans
can go back to being Republicans and Democrats to voting for
Democrats."

This is not to say that Youngdahl enjoyed a five-year political
honeymoon. Critics were not lacking who objected to what they
considered the clothing of partisan politics in the garb of moral
righteousness; others saw his tireless campaigning on the issues
of mental health, youth conservation, and law enforcement as a
convenient evasion of less dramatic but pressing governmental

problems of administrative reform, tax reform, and so on; still others, especially among conservative, economy-minded legislators, found the costs of his New Dealish social-welfare program alarming. Frustration over stubborn legislative resistance to parts of his program in 1951 may have been a factor in Youngdahl's decision to leave the governorship for the bench.

C. Elmer Anderson, who had served as lieutenant governor under Stassen, Thye, and Youngdahl, succeeded to the governorship and retained the post in the 1952 election. He continued the basic administrative policies and legislative direction set by his predecessors.

Among the veteran Republican officeholders of this era were Mike Holm, Julius A. Schmahl, and Stafford King. Holm held office as secretary of state from 1921 until his death in 1952. Schmahl served as chief clerk of the house in 1902, 1903, and 1905, as secretary of state from 1907 until 1921, and as state treasurer from 1927 until his death in 1957 (1937–39 excepted). After directing the state department of soldier welfare from 1925 to 1931, Stafford King was elected state auditor — a position he has occupied continuously since 1931. The long tenure of these officials, and, in the 1950's, the election and re-election of men like Republican Val Bjornson, state treasurer, demonstrate the tendency of Minnesota voters to keep in office men whose integrity and judgment they trust, regardless of what political winds are blowing.

Three terms under the Democratic-Farmer-Labor party, 1954–1960

The party which in 1954 brought an end to the sixteen-year Republican control of the governorship bore the label Democratic-Farmer-Labor.

In 1944 political necessity had finally effected a fusion between the two major rivals to Republicanism in the state. For twenty years there had been sporadic attempts to join Democrats and Farmer-Laborites, and since 1932 they had been united in national politics by their common support of Franklin D. Roosevelt. But there were obstacles to final union in state politics.

The Democrats were essentially an urban party. They were strong among the Irish and in the Catholic communities in St. Paul, Duluth, and St. Cloud. Their upper-middle-class leadership had conservative inclinations. To many of the Democrats, Farmer-Laborites smacked of radicalism and were too visionary for effective practical politics.

Farmer-Laborites, for their part, had reservations too. They had a strong following among the Scandinavian farmers of northwestern Minnesota and among the organized and politically conscious workers in mining, manufacturing, and railroading. Some had roots in Progressive Republicanism and felt ideologically closer to Republicans than to Democrats, whom they considered political opportunists overly concerned with federal patronage. Others were reluctant to give up the dream of a new national party unpolluted by compromise with either southern bourbons or Wall Street tycoons.

But overriding the considerations of ideology, economics, and ethnic or religious background was the pressing need to win elections. Unless these two parties could close ranks and agree on a single ticket, the Republican party would be virtually assured of continued domination of the statehouse. Only through fusion of forces, too, could maximum support for Roosevelt in 1944 be achieved; hence national Democratic leaders added their weight to the arguments for unification. Accordingly, after protracted negotiation, a new party was welded in convention early in 1944.

At that convention a leading role was taken by the man who was to become the party's top vote-getter and most prominent personality — Hubert H. Humphrey.

Humphrey was 33 years old in 1944. The preceding year he had been defeated in the Minneapolis mayoralty race and had become a political science instructor at Macalester College. After participating at the founding of the new party, he was made state DFL campaign manager for the national Roosevelt-Truman ticket. In 1945 he ran again for mayor, and was elected.

As mayor of Minneapolis (to which office he was re-elected in 1947) Humphrey earned the reputation of an effective administrator. He strengthened the role of mayor vis-à-vis the city council; he cracked down on vice, gambling, and corruption; he used to good effect citizens' volunteer committees to make recommendations on housing, veterans' affairs, fair employment practices, and law enforcement. Then in 1948 he became the first Democratic-Farmer-Labor candidate for the United States Senate.

The DFL had achieved a measure of success in 1944 and 1946, electing three of its candidates to Congress. But in 1947–48 it was rocked by one of the most bitter interparty battles in state history. It pitted left-wing supporters of Henry A. Wallace for president and Elmer Benson for senator against right-wing supporters of Harry Truman for president and Humphrey for senator. Under Humphrey's leadership, the right-wing forces, which included a large group of his former students, young business and professional men and women, labor leaders, and members of farm cooperatives, finally drove the Wallace-Benson faction from the party. Humphrey went on to rout incumbent Republican Senator Ball in the fall election, receiving nearly 60 per cent of the votes cast, and the DFL also picked up a fourth House seat.

Several of Humphrey's lieutenants in the 1947–48 party crisis became prominent DFL leaders: Eugenie Anderson, shortly to be appointed United States ambassador to Denmark; Eugene J. McCarthy, United States representative from the 4th District (St. Paul) for ten years and presently Minnesota's junior senator; Arthur Naftalin, now state commissioner of administration; and Orville L. Freeman.

A young lawyer, Freeman became state DFL chairman after the victory of the right-wing forces. As his party's candidate for governor in 1952, he lost to C. Elmer Anderson by more than 160,000 votes. But 1954 brought a sweeping victory to the DFL and Freeman, who again headed the state ticket. In that year too, the Conservatives lost control of the state house of representatives for the first time since the mid-thirties; the Liberal caucus, which organized the house, included strong DFL supporters and maintained close ties with the party. Freeman was reelected by substantial majorities in 1956 and 1958.

25

During his three terms Governor Freeman has developed effectively the technique of seeking the counsel of citizen-experts in such complex fields as taxation, government ethics, agriculture, consumer credit, and atomic development. Study committees in two fields — taxation and governmental reorganization — have conducted exhaustive surveys on the state's resources and needs. In cooperation with business interests, Freeman has initiated a vigorous "Sell Minnesota" campaign to encourage economic growth in the state and attract new business and industry. Although the Conservative-controlled senate has acted as a brake in the legislature, certain reforms advocated by the governor have been enacted: increased benefits in workmen's compensation, unemployment insurance, and old-age assistance; improvements in salary scales for public employees; establishment of a new department of corrections; authorization of reapportionment of state legislative districts; extension of the term of executive officers, including governor, to four years; a good start in revising the election, juvenile, highway, education, and probate codes.

Republican criticism of the Freeman administration has centered largely on charges of unnecessary spending; critics like George MacKinnon, who unsuccessfully opposed Freeman in the 1958 gubernatorial campaign, have also accused DFL officials of being overly friendly toward allegedly lawless elements in labor unions and of "mismanagement in the letting of government contracts."

Despite the DFL's solid successes at the polls, certain internal strains are evident — some growing out of personality conflicts, some having to do with policy differences. In the presidential primary of 1956 an inner party conflict was on public view. Freeman, Humphrey, and most of the state officials stumped vigorously on behalf of Adlai Stevenson. But a number of other party leaders — including influential state representatives Peter S. Popovich and Donald D. Wozniak of St. Paul — supported Estes Kefauver and made pointed references to "bossism" in connection with the Humphrey-Freeman attempt to marshal the state's Democrats solidly behind Stevenson. When the primary ballots were counted, it was Kefauver and not Stevenson who won the majority of district delegates to the Democratic National Convention. The DFL higher echelon smarted under the double slap from the traditionally independent electorate and from the rebellious element in its own ranks. The cleavage has left its mark on party unity, although both factions have proclaimed harmony.

The success of the DFL in maintaining (sometimes under great stress) its coalition of Farmer-Laborites, old-line Democrats, New Deal city intellectuals, and unionized workers has been attributed by its own leaders to the party's systematic use of pre-primary endorsements, which focus party energies on behalf of one candidate. On the other hand, certain old-time Farmer-Laborites consider the pre-primary endorsement an undemocratic, "palace-guard" device to control the party. It has been challenged, thus far unsuccessfully, by Paul A. Rasmussen, who opposed convention-endorsed Orville Freeman for the gubernatorial nomination in 1954, and by Hjalmar Petersen, who ran against convention-endorsed Eugene McCarthy for the 1958 senatorial nomination.

Beyond pre-primary endorsements and great organizing zeal, the DFL has a strong unifying force in the person of the state's popular senior senator. While Humphrey has developed presidential ambitions, he has attempted to avoid Stassen's mistakes and he tirelessly cultivates his grassroots support in Minnesota.

Humphrey first captured national attention while still mayor of Minneapolis, when he established the city's Fair Employment Practices Commission. As one of the "young Turks" at the 1948 Democratic National Convention he attracted further notice by his stand on civil rights. "To those who say that this civil rights program is an infringement on states' rights," Humphrey proclaimed, "I say this. The time has arrived in America for the Democratic party to get out of the shadows of states' rights and to walk forthrightly into the bright sunshine of human rights."

Freshman senators must customarily temper their oratory and eagerness somewhat, but after his re-election in 1954, Humphrey rapidly emerged from his apprenticeship to take a place on the Senate's inner council as a powerful though controversial member. His wide-ranging legislative activities and interests extend from foreign policy and social welfare to agriculture and government reform. His committee appointments (member of the Senate Foreign Relations Committee; subcommittee chairman on disarmament; subcommittee chairman on Near Eastern and African affairs) suggest the respect in which his peers hold him. His participation in the Eleventh General Assembly of the United Nations, along with his trips to the Near East and the Soviet Union, has made him one of the most internationally minded men in Washington. He has been a steady critic of the Benson farm program, a friend of the "family farm," and an advocate of organized labor and cooperatives. In his current proposal to use surplus American agricultural produce on behalf of world peace there is a neat joining of his domestic and international interests.

To his well-wishers Humphrey is one of the most effective contemporary spokesmen for the New Deal heritage, for minorities, and for social justice. Critics to the left of his own position charge him with inconsistency, if not outright failure of nerve, because of the stand he took when he gave his strong support to the Communist Control Act of 1954; the civil-rights-defender Humphrey seems to them in danger of capitulation to the presidential-aspirant Humphrey who makes friends and alliances among southern colleagues. Right-of-center observers, on the other hand, are still alarmed by his early civil rights stand, and fear that his pro-labor sympathies may lead him to work hand in glove with Walter Reuther and other labor potentates in turning the Democratic party into a labor party. Still others see in Humphrey nothing but a glib opportunist with strong demagogic inclinations.

Whatever the future course of his career, he has certainly achieved substantial stature as a senator, and his love of politics, his nimble mind and articulate tongue, his tremendous energy and intense ambition fortuitously coupled with genuine personal warmth — all these make him a formidable candidate in any political campaign and a continuing force on the Minnesota political scene.

PARTY PATTERNS, ISSUES, AND LEADERS

Party programs and prospects in the 1960's

The changing patterns in the voting strength of the major parties during the modern era in Minnesota are shown graphically in Figures 1–3. Some indication of the potential party strengths of the present may be found in statistics reported by the *Minneapolis Tribune*'s highly reliable "Minnesota Poll."* In June 1958 the Poll asked, "In politics, do you consider yourself a Democrat-Farmer-Laborite, or a Republican, or a member of some other party?" Forty-six per cent of those responding said they were Democrat-Farmer-Laborites; 34 per cent, Republicans; 15 per cent, independents; 5 per cent were undecided or refused to answer.

The mixed rural-urban party patterns in the state were also shown by the Poll results:

	DFL	Rep.	Other
Big cities	53%	24%	23%
Smaller cities	40	38	22
Towns	40	45	15
Farmers	48	33	19

DFL strength resides in the big cities, where labor unions are centered (72 per cent of the labor union members polled indicated DFL affiliation) and among farmers; in the towns and smaller cities Republicans run about even or slightly ahead.

What do these figures portend for the future?

While the DFL presently has a sizable plurality of support, the balance of power rests with the independents. The existence of this large block of voters, together with the considerable number of others who habitually split their ballots or switch party allegiances once, twice, or several times over the years, means that no party can rest on its laurels in Minnesota. As old problems persist and new needs appear, the party in office in the state, as well as the party seeking office, must adjust and adapt its program and infuse it with fresh political talent if it is to keep or gain the confidence of the electorate.

*An indication of the Poll's reliability is its record in predicting election results. In a period of eight years (1950–58) the Poll's error in seventeen contests did not exceed an average of 2.46 per cent. (*Minneapolis Tribune*, February 7, 1959.)

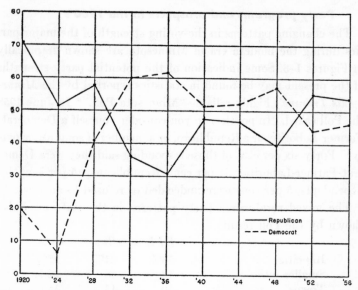

Figure 1. Percentage of Votes Cast in Minnesota for Republican
and Democratic Candidates for President, 1920–56

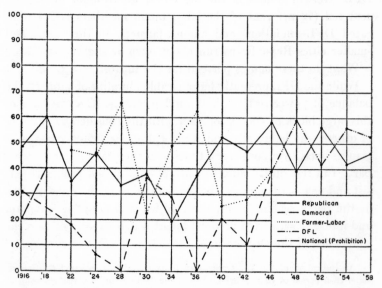

Figure 2. Percentage of Votes Cast for Senatorial Candidates
of Various Parties in Minnesota, 1916–58

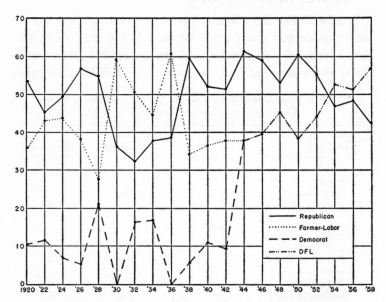

Figure 3. Percentage of Votes Cast for Gubernatorial
Candidates of the Major Parties in Minnesota, 1920–58

The basic principles that have guided each party in the recent
past, however, are likely to remain important in the 1960's, although perhaps modified in emphasis.

The Democratic-Farmer-Labor party has been closely associated with the New Deal or liberal wing of the national party.
It is committed to high and fixed agricultural supports, to the
preservation of the rights of organized labor, to a widening and
increasing of social welfare services, to a broadly internationalist
foreign policy.

The state Republican party has for the most part identified
itself with the Eisenhower national program, which while espous-
ing liberal human values, has been conservative in economic
matters and favorable toward private rather than governmental
initiative and responsibility in many areas.

On the state level the issue that has recently divided the two
parties most sharply has been that of government spending and
taxation: how much should be spent, and on what? how should

31

it be raised? The Republicans have opposed what they consider extravagance and unnecessary increase in the state debt; they have advocated a progressive sales tax (exempting certain necessities) as the soundest basis for increasing available state funds.

Table 1. Percentage of Votes Cast for Major Candidates in Mower County and in Minnesota from 1950 to 1958*

Office and Candidate	Mower County	Minnesota
1950 Election		
Governor		
Youngdahl (Rep.)	59.0%	60.7%
Peterson (DFL)	40.1	38.3
1952 Election		
President		
Eisenhower (Rep.)	53.2	55.3
Stevenson (Dem.)	46.1	44.1
Senator		
Thye (Rep.)	55.1	56.6
Carlson (DFL)	44.3	42.5
Governor		
Anderson (Rep.)	53.7	55.3
Freeman (DFL)	45.5	44.0
1954 Election		
Senator		
Humphrey (DFL)	56.1	56.4
Bjornson (Rep.)	42.8	42.1
Governor		
Freeman (DFL)	51.2	52.7
Anderson (Rep.)	48.2	46.8
1956 Election		
President		
Eisenhower (Rep.)	50.7	53.7
Stevenson (Dem.)	48.8	46.1
Governor		
Freeman (DFL)	56.5	51.4
Nelsen (Rep.)	43.1	48.2
1958 Election		
Senator		
McCarthy (DFL)	52.2	52.9
Thye (Rep.)	47.5	46.6
Governor		
Freeman (DFL)	60.5	56.8
MacKinnon (Rep.)	38.7	42.3

*Austin is the largest city in the county; the Hormel Packing Plant is its largest industry. The county's population is 54.6 per cent urban, 26.6 per cent rural-farm, and 19.8 per cent rural-nonfarm.

The percentages of the vote cast for minor candidates have not been included.

The Democrats have generally favored increased governmental services to satisfy increased needs, and they have opposed the sales tax, favoring instead a withholding plan for the state income tax.

In the 1960's this will most certainly continue to be a hotly contested political issue. There are many others. Minnesota's growing urbanization (in 1950 for the first time the state's urban population was greater than the rural) is accentuating problems in housing, education, juvenile delinquency, law enforcement, and so on. The state's expanding industrialization carries seeds of increasingly complex labor-management relations. At the same time the problems of farmers, who remain the backbone of Minnesota's economy, show no signs of lessening.

How the voters react to these issues, which of the parties' philosophies proves best suited to the times, will depend in part on largely unpredictable factors: the existence of prosperity or depression, drought or plenty, peace or war. Election victories will of course also depend in part on the public image of each of the parties as instruments of integrity and vitality — and on the influence of national and state political leaders with imagination and popular appeal.

It can safely be predicted, I think, only that Minnesota politics will continue to be vigorously combative — and often surprising.

As a footnote for would-be prognosticators, it is of interest that Minnesota has one bellwether county. Since 1950 Mower County in the 1st Congressional District has never been on the losing side. Table 1 shows how amazingly close Mower has come in "predicting" Minnesota election trends.

2

ELECTION LAW AND PARTY ORGANIZATION

Who may vote in Minnesota

UNDER the constitution and laws of this state any 21-year-old United States citizen, native or naturalized for at least three months, unless convicted of a felony or declared mentally incompetent, is eligible to vote if he has resided for six months in Minnesota and for thirty days in his precinct. In municipalities with a population of 10,000 or more, where registration is required, and in those communities under 10,000 which have voluntarily introduced a registration system, the voter must be properly registered before he can participate in elections. Residents of towns and cities where permanent registration systems are in effect make application to their respective city or town clerks (sometimes called commissioners of registration), and when once entered on the rolls need not re-register unless they fail to vote at least once in four years or they change their place of residence. Those living in areas lacking such a system may be asked, as a condition for obtaining the ballot, to take an oath that they are properly qualified.

Minnesota law permits absentee voting by its residents who are in the armed forces and by those unable to appear personally at the polls because of travel, religious holidays, or poor health.

Who may be a candidate for public office

With some exceptions, any qualified voter may also be a candidate for a state elective office. To run for governor or lieutenant governor, however, a person must be at least 25 years old and must have lived in Minnesota for at least one year preceding the

34

election. Candidates for the United States Senate must be at least 30, have been a United States citizen for nine years, and be an inhabitant of the state; the minimum age for the national House of Representatives is 25, with a minimum citizenship requirement of seven years. Under a 1956 constitutional amendment those seeking office on the state bench (the supreme, district, and probate courts), and by state law those seeking municipal judgeships, must be attorneys-at-law.

Filing for office and the preparation of ballots

Persons seeking such statewide offices as governor, treasurer, or United States senator must file affidavits of candidacy with the secretary of state during a period fixed by law but not less than 50 nor more than 90 days before the state primary election. The same procedure applies to candidacy for the United States House of Representatives (except that in the 4th and 5th Congressional districts, the candidates file with the Ramsey and Hennepin County auditors, respectively) and for the Minnesota legislature from districts comprising more than one county. Candidates to the legislature from one-county districts file with their county auditors, as do those seeking all county positions.

For all statewide and judiciary offices, the filing fee is $100. Candidates for the United States House of Representatives and Senate pay fees of $100 and $150 respectively. The filing fee for state legislature is $20; for county office, $20; for offices in cities of the first class, $10; in cities of the second and third class, $5; in cities of the fourth class, $2.

When seeking offices that carry party designation, that is, the statewide non-judicial and non-legislative posts, candidates must indicate on their affidavit their party affiliation. According to state law this means merely that a candidate, unless voting for the first time, was "affiliated with his political party at the last general election . . . [that] he voted for a majority of the candidates of the political party . . . and [that] he intends to so vote at the ensuing election." Minnesota does not provide for public registration of party membership; no formal evidence is required as to the actual association of a candidate with the party organization; and no statement of party principle or philosophy is demanded. Thus an office-seeker's claim to party affiliation may have little or no substance.

Other and even graver abuses are encouraged by such lax filing procedures. Minnesotans — and the problem is by no means unique to this state — frequently witness the spectacle of last-minute filings by candidates whose motives are unworthy of the sanctity of the ballot and the public trust. Opportunists with no chance of winning and no genuine interest in political office are attracted by the free advertising and attention a public contest affords. Others unscrupulously use the filing privilege as a means of confusing the voters. More than once a party and its candidate have been plagued by the sudden emergence of a political unknown whose only recommendation is an ethnically typical name (in Minnesota, Johnson, Peterson, and Anderson carry a certain political magic) or a name identical to that of a major contender. Even when themselves innocent, these persons may have been inveigled into "stooge" roles by factions or leaders bent on "rule or ruin" tactics. In close contests such maneuvers can easily corrupt the vote.

There can be no defense of practices which mislead the electorate, disrupt the meaningful process of choice, and destroy the very essence of an orderly election. Various legislative proposals have been introduced from time to time in an effort to curb unethical candidacies, but so far no bill has become law. One such bill, H.F. 1292, drawn in 1955 by Karl F. Grittner, state representative from the 39th district (St. Paul), would demand of any candidate for office a special statement of "intent" to be filed with the secretary of state or the county auditor not more than 120 and not less than 50 days before the primary election. Additionally, candidates would be required to file a "nominating petition" signed by a stipulated percentage of voters, the percentage varying with the type of office. In the case of statewide offices these petitions would have to show genuine geographical distribution, bearing signatures from at least five congressional districts and with no more than 25 per cent of the signatures originating in any one district. Supporters of H.F. 1292 and similar proposals contend that their admitted complexity would be well worth enduring if "stooge" and nuisance candidacies could be thereby reduced appreciably.

Minnesota law names city, village, and township clerks, county auditors, and the secretary of state as the key officials concerned with the supervision, preparation, and distribution of ballots, and charges them with the general administration of the election code. Recent statutes have increased the discretionary powers of these officials as regards the form, size, style, and type to be used in the actual printing of the ballot, but still governed by law are such matters as the position of parties on the ballot, the rotation of names, use of sample ballots, colors, and the handling of ballot errors and corrections. White ballots, for instance, are to be used only for federal and statewide candidates, pink ballots for constitutional amendments, canary-colored ballots for county offices, and light green ones for town and village offices. To avoid confusion when the last names of candidates are spelled or pronounced similarly, the law permits as additional identification a reference in not more than three words to the person's office, his residence, or his occupation.

If the governing body of any municipality so decides, voting machines may be used instead of paper ballots. The type of machines used must be approved by a three-member state voting machine commission. The law also governs such matters as the arrangement of names, provision for secrecy of the ballot, maintenance and custody of the machines, voter assistance.

Minnesota has a long ballot, and her voters sometimes endure a tedious wait during the rush hours of an election day. To an already impressive list of federal and state officials are added, with slight variation from county to county (and from one election to another in the case of staggered-term offices), some fifteen or sixteen county positions: auditor, treasurer, register of deeds, clerk of court, sheriff, attorney, judge of probate, surveyor, coroner, court commissioner, superintendent of schools, Torrens examiner, assessor, and usually two or three of the five county commissioners.

In municipal elections the length of the ballot varies from city to city. A Minneapolis voter at the 1959 general city election, for instance, was asked to vote on candidates for twenty-eight offices, on two charter amendments, and on a school referendum. In rural towns residents vote usually for one out of three supervisors, a clerk, a treasurer, an assessor, two justices of the peace, and two constables.

Primary and general elections

Minnesota now holds its primary elections for state and federal offices on the second Tuesday in September of each even-numbered year. The primary ballot includes all candidates for the United States Congress, for the state constitutional positions of governor, lieutenant governor, treasurer, auditor, secretary of state, and attorney general, for the office (created by statute) of railroad and warehouse commissioner, and for positions in the state legislature and state judiciary. (The 1959 legislature abolished the presidential preference primary law enacted in 1949. It had provided that candidates for nomination for the office of president could file either by an affidavit or by a petition bearing the signatures of 100 voters of the party in each congressional district. The leadership of both parties had suffered embarrassing experiences during the life of the law — the Republicans in 1952, the Democrat-Farmer-Laborites in 1956.)

It was the "muckrakers" and reformers at the turn of the century who vehemently demanded public primaries conducted with secrecy, privacy, and opportunity for rank-and-file participation. In Minnesota the legislative history of the primary election begins with a law of 1899, which was applicable to Hennepin County only (city and county judicial candidates and candidates for school and park boards); in 1901 it was extended as a mandatory act throughout the state. In 1912 the legislature added state constitutional offices to the primary ballot. It is interesting to note that the 1912 measure grew out of political expedience:

forces opposed to incumbent Governor Adolph O. Eberhart controlled the party convention and the governor's supporters felt that their candidate would fare better in a popular primary. After 1913 state legislators, county officials, and elected officials in cities of the first class also appeared on the primary ballot.

The consolidated primary ballot law was not adopted until 1933. Under its provisions the voter need not reveal his partisanship in any way, since a single ballot contains the names of all candidates for party-designated offices, arranged in separate columns according to party affiliation. The voter chooses among those who have filed for each office under his party's label the one he favors as that party's candidate for the ensuing general election; while he may of course abstain from voting for certain offices he may not "split" his vote by wandering into the other party's set of candidates, on penalty of nullifying his entire ballot.

Along with this consolidated party ballot the voter also receives a primary ballot for non-party-designated offices. In such contests the two top-runners for each office become the winners of the primary election and the contestants in the ensuing general election. If there happen to be, for example, seven primary candidates for the non-party-designated position of representative to the state legislature from the 44th district, five of these seven will be "weeded out" while the two top vote-getters will go on to battle it out in November.

The contests for party-designated offices are also usually between two candidates in the general election — one Republican meeting one DFL rival. However, participation by third parties and even by "lone wolves" is not precluded. Minnesota law enables groups too small to qualify as parties, and also individuals without any formal party support, to enter a general election by means of nominating petitions carrying a stipulated number of signatures, based on a percentage of the vote cast for the same office at the last general election. Write-in votes are also legal in general elections, and although some voters write in their own names, or Marilyn Monroe's, a vital civil right is preserved thereby.

39

Elections and the counting of votes

As in most of the other states, general statewide elections are held the first Tuesday following the first Monday in November of each even-numbered year. Ballots for federal and state offices are cast and counted in 3,790 precincts throughout the state. Polls remain open from 7:00 A.M. to 8:00 P.M.; notices giving the location of the precinct polling place and other pertinent information must be posted by the town, village, or city clerks at least fifteen days before both primary and general elections.

Municipal elections, primary and general, are customarily held at times governed by charter or general law. Annual village elections usually come on the first Tuesday after the first Monday in November or December, whereas most independent school district elections fall on the third Tuesday in May. Annual town meetings convene on the second Tuesday in March.

Election judges are appointed by municipal councils or county boards, with a minimum of three for each precinct. Each political party must be represented. In elections involving party-designated offices "the chairman of an authorized committee of each political party" may in writing present the name of a "challenger," who is then permitted to remain in the polling place. Either he or any one of the election judges may insist that persons with dubious qualifications who refuse to cooperate or decline to take an oath affirming the sufficiency of their qualifications be barred from voting under the terms of the election code.

How ballots are to be counted, how they are to be tallied, stored, and sealed, what is meant by a defective vote, and how election results are to be forwarded to the canvassing boards — all these operations are prescribed by state law. A county canvassing board includes the county auditor, the clerk of district court, two members from the county board, and the mayor of the most populous city. This board forwards to the secretary of state a certificate indicating the number of votes cast and counted and the results by precinct for each office, constitutional amendment, and other issue submitted to the voters. If a tie vote occurs the canvassing board may decide the outcome by lot; whenever election judges are suspected of error, the board may, if four-fifths of its members so vote, inspect a precinct's ballots. At the apex of the state election machinery stands the five-member State Canvassing Board, consisting of the secretary of state together with two district and two supreme court justices. This agency formally reports and certifies the official vote in a primary or general election.

Anti-corrupt practices laws

In order to ensure honest elections, the legislature under its police power has from time to time passed statutes regulating the conduct of campaigns. Political advertising and campaign literature must be properly labeled and identified; candidates and their supporters may not legally exert undue influence on voters or compel them to vote or to abstain from voting; no public or private promises may be given in exchange for a vote or as a promotional device; corporations are prohibited from making monetary contributions or from furnishing the "free service of [their] officers or employees." The purposes for which expenditures may be legally authorized are specified by law and include, among other items, office and hall rents, the printing of pamphlets, posters, handbills, and other campaign literature, filing fees, advertising expenses, and the candidate's personal travel, telephone, telegraph, and postal expenditures. Disbursements are allowable for expenses incurred by campaign organizers and committee members. Expenditure limits are fixed at $7,000 for gubernatorial candidates, at $3,500 for those seeking the other statewide constitutional offices, at $800 and $600 for candidates to the state senate and the state house of representatives respectively. Central committees of the political parties are held to a $10,000 maximum for the entire ticket.

Obviously these sums, set in 1917, won't buy much of a campaign today. As a matter of fact they have been circumvented legally and effectively, as for example by the activities of so-called "volunteer" or "political" committees. Enjoying freedom from fixed statutory limits on expenditures and receipts, such committees may, according to judicial interpretations and rulings by various attorneys general, collect and spend funds to the extent of their ambition or ability. Volunteer committees and their candidates thus acquire influence and financial power at the expense of the party organizations, whose fiscal activities are so much more carefully restricted. The major parties and most of their candidates have long favored raising the statutory limits to a more realistic level.

In Florida, where fiscal limits on committees have been removed altogether, candidates may spend money without restriction but they must make periodic public accounting of the source and disposition of campaign funds. In addition Florida requires that all financial transactions pass through the hands of a publicly announced campaign treasurer (selected by the candidate himself), that all contributions be kept in a special bank account, and that no payments be made by anyone without a formal voucher submitted to the campaign treasurer for his approval.

The Florida experiment, while only one of various approaches to the tremendously complex interplay of money and politics, has been viewed with considerable interest; it is among the possibilities now under study by the Minnesota Interim Commission on Election Law.

Parties and party organizations

Although only 22 of the approximately 32,500 local, state, and federal offices on Minnesota ballots carry party designation, these 22 include such important posts as those of United States senator, United States representative, state governor, other state constitutional officers, and (in presidential years) president and vice president.

These are the prizes for which the parties struggle as they recruit candidates, fight campaigns, write platforms, arouse the enthusiasm of their own supporters, and attempt to make converts from the opposition and from those who classify themselves as "independents." Despite the impressive roles they play, there is not a single word in either the state or federal constitution referring to political parties and their functions. Courts in Minnesota and in other states, however, have held the organization of political parties to be an inherent right of citizenship. Like any other right it is not absolute, but may under certain circumstances be made subject to legislative control.

Under Minnesota law a political group in order to be recognized as a legitimate party must operate a statewide organization and must have presented in every county one or more candidates who polled at least 5 per cent of the total vote cast at the last general election. Parties may also obtain a place on the primary election ballot by a petition to the county auditor containing signatures numbering at least 5 per cent of the total vote cast at the last general election in the county.

The law forbids the theft of names of already existing parties, nor may any part of a current party label be appropriated by any other party or candidate. In view of Minnesota's history of third parties and of hyphenated parties which have resulted from the marriage of once-separate factions, this concern for the integrity of party labels is no mere technicality. Without legal prohibitions, a splinter group or a dissident candidate could gain votes, or at least confuse and mislead the electorate, by using such appelations as "Democratic-Labor," "Farmer-Labor-Republican," or simply "Democratic" alone. In the 1953 legislative session a quiet effort was made by some anti-Humphrey forces to amend the law and permit appropriation of another party's name. What this would mean in a closely fought contest, if for example a Democratic ticket were placed alongside a Democratic-Farmer-Labor ticket, is not too difficult to imagine. Fortunately for party "regulars" the bill died in the closing hours of the session.

Under the terms of the 1959 election code final legal authority over the internal affairs of each political party is lodged in the state convention it must hold at least once every general election year. These conventions may be considered the highest legislative assemblies of the parties. Between sessions of the convention, "subject to the control of the state convention," as the law puts it, the state central committee is invested by the election code with power over a party's affairs.

Within their broad statutory framework parties work out their own constitutions, promulgate rules, and perform all the other tasks required of self-governing organizations. Despite important differences in outlook and perhaps even in composition, the organizations of the major parties are very similar.

Precinct caucus and county, district, and state conventions

To the average citizen, the precinct or township caucus is the most significant of the several party assemblies. Here, on the lowest stratum in the party pyramid, is the arena where the rank and file of party membership — the perhaps ten or fifteen voters in the neighborhood (out of perhaps fifty) who consider themselves politically active — meet at least once every other year in order to perform important party business. At the caucus, delegates to county conventions are chosen, the precinct's own committee officers are elected, party policies and personalities are discussed, rejected, and endorsed.

Thus action taken on the precinct level carries decisive implications for the party as a whole. Yet Minnesota belongs to that group of states which demand only the most minimal and subjective tests as prerequisites to caucus participation. A voter's statement that he supported, voted with, or affiliated with the party in the past, that he agrees with its principles as stated in the party constitution, and that he promises future support — only such generalized affirmations are required of him. And since his support may well have been confined to the privacy of the polling booth and the secret ballot, external verification is difficult. If challenged, however, an individual's right to participate may be put to a vote by the precinct caucus.

The law has singled out these primary party meetings for careful attention — and with good reason, since precinct "raiding," when carried out systematically and by design, can put an entire party in danger of seizure from within by elements completely antagonistic to its established principles. A political party, it should be remembered, is something more than a mere private club transacting private business; a party's choice of candidates and its endorsement of policies have ramifications for the entire body politic. Hence the legislature is rightfully concerned that the precinct caucus should be convened and conducted with fairness and with certain procedural safeguards.

The law prescribes that the "call" (the formal document sent out by the county chairman of the party announcing the precinct caucuses) must indicate (in addition to the date, time, and location) the number of delegates to be elected, the nature of the business to be transacted, and the names of the precinct and county chairman. Space is provided on the back of the "call" for the names and addresses of the delegates elected to the county conventions. This facilitates the issuing of credentials by the county chairmen to the newly elected delegates.

Precinct caucus and precinct organization have properly been called the backbone of party structure. If the local party workers slacken their efforts or if they incorrectly reflect public sentiment, campaign goals are jeopardized and elections may be lost. On the other hand an active local organization can do much to bring new recruits and resources to the party. Many an election has been won or lost by the degree of enthusiasm with which precinct workers distributed literature, placed posters, collected money, organized house-to-house canvasses, sponsored coffee parties, conducted telephone drives, and performed the myriad of other tasks without which campaigns are rarely successful. For best results, of course, precinct activities must be integrated into the county and statewide campaign strategy so as to avoid duplication of effort.

In the cities all the precincts located within a "ward"—a somewhat flexible area which in Minneapolis constitutes an aldermanic district—may wish to form a ward club. Joint party educational programs and "socials" can often further the effectiveness of the local organization and help in its campaign tasks.

Generally, precinct delegates make up the membership of county conventions, county delegates the congressional district conventions, and county and district delegates the state convention. In conventions at the county level and above, both of the major parties determine the number of delegates from each lower unit by apportionment formulas, based usually on party vote in the precinct, county, or district at the last election. Certain party officials, however, become delegates ex officio.

To give their party greater organizational continuity and stability, Republicans made a number of important constitutional changes in 1959. Instead of meeting biennially as specified earlier, county and district conventions are directed to assemble every year, and district conventions and county conventions may elect their officers in odd-numbered years. The regular DFL conventions all meet only in election years, although there may be "extraordinary" conventions called at other times.

The county, district, and state conventions follow the precinct caucuses at two- or three-week intervals; their structure and order of business are somewhat similar. After the customary invocations, speeches of welcome, and announcements comes the first important issue: the seating of delegates. This is accomplished by adopting the report of the Credentials Committee, a group which along with several other appointed committees (as for example Platform, Rules, Resolutions, Nominations, Constitution, Endorsements, Arrangements) has convened in advance of the convention itself. Given party harmony, the work of the Credentials Committee is little more than a routine scrutiny of the delegates' certificates; but on occasion seats are bitterly contested, especially if irregularities occurred at lower conventions or if intraparty disputes have produced rival slates with opposing claims of legitimacy. In such cases the faction dominating the Credentials Committee may in effect steer the outcome of the convention itself.

Perhaps second in significance to the Credentials Committee is the Committee on Rules. Its report, when adopted by the convention, governs the agenda or order of business, defines the procedure for formal voting and other parliamentary practice (as for example the number and length of seconding speeches, or the allocation of voting power in case of absences in a delegation), stipulates the circumstances under which a roll call may be demanded, sets the quorum required for floor business, and — unless provided for specifically in the party's state constitution — decides the conditions under which the convention may endorse candidates for public office.

Once properly organized, the convention gets down to business, for it must elect convention officers and party officers, choose delegates for the next higher convention, perhaps make amendments to the party constitution, and come to decisions regarding the party's platform and policy. Often its most touchy business concerns the endorsement of candidates.

Heated debates over endorsement have given the conventions of the Democratic-Farmer-Labor party an air of suspense and drama, as well as considerable publicity. The issue is joined, as we saw in Chapter 1, between those in favor of pre-primary party endorsement of particular candidates, and those opposed. Proponents of pre-primary endorsement stress the need for party unity in the primaries; they argue that financial and organizational resources can be used to better advantage in fighting "the enemy" than in family quarrels; they reason that early endorsements produce strong, responsible, balanced party tickets committed to the support of party platform and principle; they claim too that campaigns are most effective when all members of the ticket support each other and reinforce each other's appeal. Voters, they argue, will be less open to exploitation by high-pressure personalities, "beauty" contests, stooge candidacies, and irresponsible appeals when they have the counsel of professionals who have looked over the field and approved the most reliable and promising candidates. Since serious misjudgments in endorsement are very injurious to the party's chances in the general election, the party leaders are likely to be very careful. And after all, they conclude, there still remains the public primary, at which voters may turn down party recommendations and thus register grassroots protest when it appears that the "regulars" have made a mistake.

Opponents of pre-primary party endorsement rest their case squarely on what they insist is the heart and spirit of the primary as a device, designed by reformers and independents, to wrest the power to nominate candidates from the hands of bosses, machines, and party organizations, and return it to the rank and file, who can then vote for their candidates rather than for those chosen for them by the "professionals." Through pre-primary endorsements, parties *tell* the voter for whom to vote rather than *ask* him whom he wants as his nominee. Who is better entitled to voice the sentiments of the party than the majority of individual members who cast their votes in the secrecy of the primary? And should not the nonconforming political figure who is out of favor with the party "palace guard" have an opportunity to put the strength of his personality and conviction to the test of rank-and-file vote? They might decide he can best minister to party ills.

Democratic-Farmer-Labor leaders around Senator Hubert Humphrey, Governor Orville Freeman, and Senator Eugene J. McCarthy have always considered the pre-primary endorsement a *sine qua non* for building a responsible and effective party program, for conducting successful campaigns whether the office is state or federal, legislative or executive. Despite bitter internal struggles and slow beginnings, the DFL party has been rather successful in utilizing the pre-primary endorsement, for since its fusion in 1944 it has been able to carry nearly four out of five endorsed candidates successfully through the primary elections.

The tradition against official pre-primary endorsement is much stronger in the Republican party. In part because of rural fears of urban-dominated party councils, perhaps in part because of the influence of strong personalities irrevocably opposed to party endorsement, various moves to adopt this practice suffered repeated defeats during the 1940's and 1950's. However, in 1959 the party took a step in the direction of pre-primary endorsement when it amended its constitution to permit such endorsements.

Under the present provision, a convention may by vote of 60 per cent of the delegates (rather than the two-thirds vote required in the DFL) give pre-primary endorsement to candidates for the United States Senate and for those state offices carrying party designation. However, "[w]hen more than one such candidate is nominated for endorsement, none of them shall be voted upon separately and the candidacy of all shall be submitted on each ballot."

State central and executive committees

During the intervals between state conventions each party functions through its central and executive committees.

Meeting two or more times a year, the central committee of each party has between 200 and 300 members and includes the major leadership of the party. Among the members are the state executive officers (chairman, chairwoman, vice chairman, vice chairwoman, secretary, and treasurer), the corresponding executive officers of county and district organizations, the national committeeman and committeewoman, representatives of the party's nominees for major state and federal office, county delegations (in addition to county officers), and the executive officers of such auxiliaries as the Young Republican League, Federation of College Republican Clubs, Federation of Women's Republican Clubs, and the Young Democratic-Farmer-Labor clubs. Delegates may be sent to represent those state constitutional offices currently held by the party. The DFL admits delegates sent by the Liberal members of the Minnesota legislature, and in addition it seats its immediate past chairman and chairwoman.

In both parties the executive committee is a smaller group of usually 30 to 65 persons, among them the state executive officers, the national committeeman and committeewoman, the nine district chairmen and chairwomen, and other party leaders appointed by the chairman or elected at large by party groups at the county, district, and state levels. Meeting as often as once a month, the executive committee carries out the policies of the state convention and the state central committee; its chairman,

49

who also chairs the central committee, is known as the chairman of the party. Among other duties the executive committee maintains a party headquarters where the party's day-to-day activities in public relations, finance, and organization are handled by a small full-time staff. In recent years the work of political parties in Minnesota and elsewhere has become so heavy as to require the services of an executive secretary. Such salaried officials (at present Clyne Olson for the DFL and Herbert O. Johnson for the Republicans) are appointed by the state chairman with the advice and consent of the executive or central committee.

In a politically competitive state like Minnesota state chairmen and executive directors face constant challenge. Organizational and publicity problems must be solved or elections will be lost. Inactive county and district groups must be rebuilt, family quarrels smoothed over, new members recruited, finances kept on a solid footing, and so on. Precinct, county, and district efforts must be integrated into the state strategy. Membership lists and voter registration must be kept up to date, money collected, patronage problems settled, disaffected officers replaced, vacancies filled. The party executive must meanwhile get favorable newspaper coverage for his party's activities and must keep the opposition's moves under scrutiny and criticism. Whether the legislature is in session or not, whether the party is in office or not, these party executives must meet an unending series of demands for leadership and conciliation, for information and favor, for assistance and counsel.

Among the Republican chairmen of the last two decades, R. C. Radabaugh, Bernhard LeVander, P. Kenneth Peterson, and John Hartle are especially remembered for their long service and influence on their party. All were connected with the Stassen administrations: Radabaugh as Stassen's campaign manager, LeVander as state director of social welfare, Hartle as a Stassen spokesman in the state house of representatives, and Peterson (the current mayor of Minneapolis) as a state legislator. The present chairman, Ed Viehman, a business associate of Dan C. Gainey, influential Republican from Owatonna, was chosen in

January of 1959 after the election of his predecessor, Ancher Nelsen, to Congress. Viehman had managed successfully two congressional campaigns for Albert H. Quie of the 1st District and is believed to reflect the more conservative thought in the party. Prominent Republican chairwomen of the same era include Mrs. Marge Howard of Excelsior, Mrs. Rhoda Lund of Minneapolis, and Mrs. Kay Harmon of St. Paul. Mrs. Evelyn Heberling (Winona) is the present chairwoman.

Orville L. Freeman, state DFL chairman from 1948 to 1950, was succeeded by Karl F. Rolvaag. He in turn was followed by Ray Hemenway of Albert Lea when the DFL swept into office in 1954 and Freeman became governor, Rolvaag lieutenant governor. Working closely with the Humphrey-Freeman leadership in the late 1940's and early 1950's was the state chairwoman, Dorothy Houston Jacobson of Minneapolis. Like Humphrey a former political science professor, Mrs. Jacobson has long been identified with the cooperative movement and with liberal politics; she was a major tactician in the struggle against the left-wing forces in the DFL; and she has become respected perhaps more than any other single person in the party as a consultant on policy. Adrian Winkel (St. Paul) and Mrs. Evelyn Malone (Windom) are the present chairman and chairwoman.

Special projects and party finance

If voters feel that their political party is a mere patronage mill, or if they feel that it keeps watch over them with the unfriendly and dictatorial mien of the "Big Brother" in Orwell's *1984*, they will sooner or later lose their loyalty and enthusiasm. The party will then sicken and elections will be lost. Accordingly, a party must recognize its responsibility to serve as a forum for mature deliberation of meaningful issues. For example, two district organizations might jointly sponsor a regional conference to deal with agriculture, labor, health, or leadership training. When the legislature is in session, party "workshops" might study and criticize current issues and bills. As the DFL leadership demonstrated during two recent sessions, the intensity of public opinion can thus be effectively impressed on the lawmakers. For a "The People Speak" conference, the Republicans sent out invitations to hundreds of groups and organizations throughout the state, soliciting their opinions on such issues as agriculture, conservation, civil rights, education, foreign affairs, human welfare, small business, industry, and labor.

For any such special projects and, of course, on a much larger scale, for election campaigns, political parties must have financial resources. Because literature, staff, newsletters, radio and television time, newspaper advertising, and other campaign requirements cost enormously, no party or candidate has ever felt that there were sufficient funds to do the job. Much of the party's energy must go into money-raising. First, each party through its finance committee and finance director seeks out individuals and organizations friendly to its program and candidates; second, there are money-raising rallies such as the Republicans' Lincoln Day dinner and the Jefferson-Jackson Day dinner of the DFL; third, there are the less formal "Fun Fests," "Bean Feeds," "Neighbor to Neighbor" drives, appreciation banquets, and so forth. The DFL makes collections through its sustaining membership plan, under which a member may contribute as little as $1.00 per month; $2.50 or more per month gives him an annual subscription to the nationwide *Democratic Digest* and also one $25 ticket to the Jefferson-Jackson Day dinner. The Republicans too use a pledge and a sustaining fund system.

Such are some methods for raising money, but what of the sources of funds? Large contributors still pay the major share of party expenses. Fund raisers on both the state and national levels agree that at least 90 per cent of the money comes from not more than 1 per cent of the population, that about 60 per cent of the amount contributed comes in denominations of $500 or over, and only 20 per cent in sums under $100. With campaign funds an object of suspicion and disdain in American politics, evoking memories of "bought" elections and "kept" candidates, political parties in Minnesota and other states must find new ways to convince the average citizen that his financial support, as a material accompaniment to his political convictions, is a practical and perhaps an ethical imperative.

The question, then, is how to broaden the base of campaign financing by getting the thousands of average citizens who have never made a contribution in the past to give financial support to the party of their choice and to back up the campaigns, candidates, and causes in which they believe. A prominent DFL leader, Byron G. Allen, has been instrumental in two pioneering experiments in Minnesota that have attacked this problem.

The first of these resulted in a law (passed in 1955) permitting any individual (corporations excepted) to deduct from his taxable net income contributions of up to $100 to political parties, candidates, or groups. Party officials may claim sums of up to $1,000, depending upon the office, as credits against taxable net income. Candidates for any public office may deduct from their gross income specified amounts ranging up to $5,000 for a United States senator or state governor.

The second experiment was encouraged by Senators Thye and Humphrey, by the national committee chairmen of both major parties, by various Washington political figures, by the editor of the Washington *Post* and *Times Herald*, and locally by the Advertising Council of Alexandria, Minnesota, and the *Park Region Echo*, the weekly newspaper of that city. In May 1956 Alexandria was the site of a bipartisan mass appeal for political funds; during three evenings teams of Democratic and Republican canvassers (going jointly from door to door) approached 1,000 voters (the population was 6,300) and collected $1,200. Seventy-six per cent of those approached made a contribution. This wide response indicated the possibilities for broadening the base of campaign contributions; it also showed that in a small town at least, the voters are not particularly eager to be publicly identified with a party. It was reported that only 20 persons chose to specify that their contributions go to a particular party.

Such an experiment, although so far not repeated, may set the fashion for future fund drives on the national level. Meanwhile campaign oratory and partisan recriminations continue to label the Republicans the "big money" party, and to imply that the DFL, dominated by "bosses" and labor money, uses Tammany methods to extort its campaign funds from unwilling workers.

State-national party links

A conspicuous feature of the American party system is the looseness of party organization on the national level. Neither the Republican nor the Democratic party is nationally much more than an association or confederation of autonomous state units. Subject of course to state and federal statutory limitations, the final authority over the internal affairs of Minnesota parties remains within the state and in the parties' own state conventions. Each party's national committee serves as a sort of liaison council during the interim between national conventions, preparing for these conventions, coordinating campaign activities, supervising the party's Washington administrative headquarters, and assisting with patronage clearances whenever the party's candidate is in the White House. Since so much of the party's organizational work and power rests, however, on the state level, the national committeemen and committeewomen sent by Minnesota and the other states might be thought of as "ambassadors" speaking for the state party organizations by whom they are elected and to whom they are responsible.

Although meeting regularly only three or four times a year, the members of the parties' national committees perform essential functions. When a Republican occupies the White House, members of the Republican National Committee are consulted or expect to be consulted about patronage, campaign tactics, and party finance. On occasion they may assist in persuading a reluctant congressman to see things the administration way. During a Democratic administration the Democratic National Committee serves similarly as liaison between Washington and the state organizations.

In addition to its regular National Committee the Democrats have another influential national group — the National Advisory Council, sometimes called the party's "liberal conscience," which often acts as a counterpoise to the conservative southern wing of the party. Minnesota has been strongly represented in the group (which includes such respected figures as Mrs. Franklin D. Roosevelt, Walter Reuther, Adlai Stevenson, Paul Douglas, and Michigan's Governor G. Mennen Williams) by Senator Humphrey, Governor Freeman, and a long-time party leader, Mrs. Ione Hunt of Montevideo. Mrs. Hunt succeeded to the post of national committeewoman when Mrs. Eugenie Anderson of Red Wing was appointed by President Truman as this nation's first woman ambassador to Denmark in 1949. Gerald W. Heaney succeeded Byron G. Allen in 1955 when Allen was appointed commissioner of agriculture. Ray Hemenway and Mrs. Geri Joseph (Minneapolis) became the National Committee members in 1960.

On the Republican side Roy E. Dunn, veteran member of the Minnesota house and its long-time majority leader, served as national committeeman for sixteen years. "Mr. Republican," as his friends like to call him, was a strong Taft supporter and a frequent vigorous opponent of Stassen's views. Mrs. Elizabeth Heffelfinger of Wayzata, at one time a Stassen supporter and a ten-year national committeewoman, has along with George W. Etzell of Clarissa (Dunn's successor in 1952) played an effective part in the Republican national organization. Etzell is presently chairman of the Rules Committee, while Mrs. Heffelfinger chaired the Committee on Arrangements for the 1956 Republican National Convention and has been secretary to the executive committee of the National Committee. Mrs. Rhoda Lund was elected national committeewoman in 1960.

In a presidential election year the national convention is the last and highest in the sequence of party assemblies which began at the grassroots with precinct caucuses. Such a convention is of course a major undertaking, involving not only immediately practical considerations — feeding and housing thousands of delegates and visitors, arranging for press, radio, and television coverage, furnishing headquarters space and staff for the would-be candidates — but also the maintaining of a community of purpose in the face of strenuous rivalries, and the presentation, to millions of Americans who act as the audience, of a viable party "image."

Even more than at the state level, the make-up of national pre-convention committees has tremendous consequences for the party as a whole. Presidential nominations and the party platform may well depend on the seating or rejection of certain delegations, on the establishment of certain rules of order, on the ideological fervor of certain committees. It is the national committee and its chairman who stand close to the sources of power and who influence appointments to the Rules and Platform and Credentials committees.

Its nominees chosen and its platform written, the national convention adjourns and party activity reverts to the state and local level. Both parties' national committee members set themselves to the task of coordinating their state campaigns with the nation-wide design. Among other things, they make every effort to have their state included in the speaking itinerary of the nominees. More because of its location and its representativeness than because of its electoral weight, Minnesota has heard a number of major campaign addresses in the past. Both Stevenson and Eisenhower delivered important policy statements on agriculture at Kasson, Minnesota, in 1956. Harry Truman made a belligerent indictment of the 80th Congress at St. Paul in 1948. Also in 1948 Minneapolis heard Henry Wallace condemn both major parties and call for a new political alignment.

To make maximum political capital of such speeches, to use all other means to rally the doubtful and keep the already loyal active — this is the job of precinct, county, district, and state party organizations, in Minnesota as in the other states.

3

A NONPARTISAN PARTISAN LEGISLATURE

WITH the single exception of Nebraska's unicameral legislature, Minnesota's is presently the only state legislature whose membership is elected on a ballot without designation as to political party. Party designation was dropped in 1913 largely as the result of a parliamentary struggle between the "drys" and the "wets" in which the opponents of prohibition working with liquor interests exploited sentiments within the legislature that were strongly critical of party machines and boss control. One must remember that this was the era of progressivism, when parties were disdained and political independence was extolled, and when it was hoped that direct political action by the people (through such means as the initiative, referendum, recall, and direct primary) would lead to more responsible government.

Political history since the early part of this century has thrown some doubt on the efficacy of these devices; it no longer seems axiomatic that the weakening of political parties serves the ends of good government. Already in 1913 voices of doubt were raised. After the Minnesota senate had added the nonpartisan feature to the primary election law, commentator Charles B. Cheney, a supporter of nonpartisanship on the local level, wrote in the *Minneapolis Journal* that "the Minnesota plan throws the door open to the nominations of the liquor and other interests as they find it easy to juggle the contests once they have degenerated into mere personal struggles."

The debate over the desirability or undesirability of party labels for legislators has since then been one of the constants in

Minnesota politics. The problem becomes ever more acute as the increasing power of the modern legislature affects larger numbers of people over wider areas of their lives.

Legislators and legislative organization

Minnesota with its 131 representatives and 67 senators has the largest senate and twelfth largest house in the nation. Representatives stand for election every two years, senators every four (in non-presidential election years). They receive salaries ranking well up among the upper fourth of those paid to legislators throughout the United States.

It may be of interest to note certain characteristics of the members of the 1959 legislature.

The occupations of the legislators varied somewhat between the two houses. In the senate 35.8 per cent were lawyers, 25.3 per cent farmers, and 19.4 per cent businessmen. In the house 22.9 per cent were lawyers, 30.5 per cent farmers, and 24.4 per cent businessmen. ("Business" here includes insurance and real estate.) In religion there were the following major groupings: Lutherans, 67; Roman Catholics, 43; Presbyterians, 24; Methodists, 20; Congregationalists, 11; and Jews, 1. In age, there was no notable difference between the two chambers; the average age in the house was 49.7 years, in the senate 51.5.

The extent of the legislators' previous experience is shown in Table 2. It is quite apparent that since 1951 important changes have occurred in the membership of the senate. In that year more

Table 2. Percentage of Legislators with Given Previous
Experience in the Legislature

No. of Terms	1893	1909	1925	1935	1951	1959
One previous term or none						
Senate	74%	15%	13%	22%	29%	60%
House	82	54	54	19	38	26
Three or more previous terms						
Senate	21	59	81	49	54	24
House	5	27	32	53	47	41

Source: Expanded from data in William P. Tucker, "Characteristics of State Legislators," *Social Science*, 30:94–98 (April 1955), p. 96.

than half of its members had served three or more terms; in 1959 three-fifths of the senators were freshmen or had only one term of previous service. Thus there was in the 1959 session a high concentration of experience and power in a relatively small group of key senators with long seniority. In this connection it is interesting that in 1950 Minnesota was the only state in which not a single committee chairmanship in either house or senate was given to a member who had served less than four terms.

In addition to considering and acting on bills, a modern state legislature must discharge a multitude of other duties in connection with its role as agent or "check and balance" for the executive and judicial branches and for local government units. These include such actions as confirming gubernatorial appointments, determining legislative contests, proposing amendments to the constitution, conducting hearings and investigations, and providing for interim legislative committees and commissions. Before it can do all this, the legislature must of course bring itself into parliamentary order by electing presiding officers, selecting committee members, determining rules, and agreeing to a calendar. Obviously a group of several dozen legislators would be unable to function unless it employed some kind of "team" structure permitting men of similar interests or aims to act as a unit, at least in formal aspects of the legislative "game." Instead of the Republican-Democratic bifurcation characteristic of other states, the Minnesota house and senate divide themselves into Liberal and Conservative caucuses. Nominations are made by each caucus for the key positions of speaker of the house and president pro tem of the senate.

The group which can command a majority of legislators' votes and so elect its candidates in either senate or house is known as the majority caucus in that chamber. This is where much of the legislative power resides, for in Minnesota the winner takes all. The winning caucus through its election of the majority leader and speaker or president pro tem controls the chairmanships and memberships of legislative committees and through the Rules Committee directs the general flow of legislative business. The parliamentary powers of the speaker of the house are particularly extensive: he appoints all the standing committees of that body, "signs all acts, addresses, joint resolutions, writs, warrants and subpoenas," prepares schedules of committee meetings, designates the chief sergeant-at-arms, and refers bills, after their first reading, to appropriate committees.

Senior members of the majority caucus chair such key committees as Finance (senate) or Appropriations (house), Taxes, Highways, Education, Labor, Public Welfare, Judiciary, Civil Administration, and Agriculture. Here bills are shaped into final form, hearings are held that focus attention and support, and administrative departments attempt to justify their programs and budgets.

In the past four decades, the Conservatives have been in firm control of the senate. The Liberals have controlled the house only in 1933, 1937, 1955, 1957, and 1959.

From positions of floor and committee leadership Conservatives like Roy Dunn (majority leader in the house for nine of the sixteen sessions he has served — longer than anyone else in the history of the state), Charles N. Orr (majority leader in the senate for five special and nine regular sessions), A. J. Rockne ("watchdog of the treasury" and twenty-year chairman of the senate Finance Committee), Donald O. Wright (a thirty-year veteran and chairman of the senate Tax Committee since 1951), and Gordon Rosenmeier (chairman of Civil Administration and influential member of the senate Conservative caucus since 1941) have fought hard and effectively against executive and legislative proposals that seemed to them "too costly," "too liberal," "too untried," or "too dangerous." Some of these men skirmished with Christianson and Stassen, some of them campaigned against the Youngdahl program, most of them fought the Olson, Benson, and Freeman administrations. Some opposed any measures strengthening the governorship or centralizing the administration; others objected to tax increases and the adoption of an income tax; some rejected expansion of government services and government regulation; not a few of them viewed with alarm the rise of organized labor and the intervention of government in new socioeconomic areas. All have stood for the constitution as framed, for the rights of property and the sanctity of contracts, for the preservation of the *status quo* — which in their judgment best assures continuation of the traditions of American freedom and individualism. And in their continued re-election they have seen proof that their constituents deem their positions worthy of support.

In the senate the citadel of present Conservative leadership is the Committee on Committees headed by Wright. On this committee sit the chairmen of such other vital committees as Finance, Taxes, Transportation, General Legislation, Judiciary, Labor, Civil Administration, Public Welfare, Rules, and Elections. The chairmen making up this committee in the 1959 session were all Conservatives. They represented all nine congressional districts, and had an average of seventeen years' legislative experience and an average age of sixty. Another Conservative bastion, likewise restricted to the majority caucus, is the Committee on Rules and Legislative Expense chaired by majority leader John M. Zwach. Though other important committees are not altogether closed to the minority caucus, that group is allotted far less than proportional representation. For example, the Liberals in 1959 held 5 of the 19 seats on the Tax Committee, 5 of 17 on Civil Administration, and 9 of 19 on the less-strategic Game and Fish Committee. This "closed" committee system is a perennial point of dispute between the two caucuses, as is the prerogative now held by the Conservatives of naming all committee appointments, including those from Liberal ranks.

In the Liberal-controlled house the Conservatives in 1959 were excluded from the Rules Committee but held 13 of 29 seats on Appropriations and a similar quota of seats on the Tax Committee. In part this more generous arrangement is explained by the near equality of the two caucuses in the house (59 Conservatives, 72 Liberals) as compared with the heavily Conservative complexion of the senate (43 Conservatives, 24 Liberals). In addition, house committee procedure is governed by a 1957 rules amendment (sponsored by the Liberals) which directs the speaker to "give due consideration" to committee preferences of the minority caucus "with the end in view of attaining a proportionate representation on such committees for the minority group."

The house Liberal majority have bitterly criticized the Conservatives in control of the senate for dragging their heels on reform measures, for blocking or slowing down legislative action considered essential by the Liberals. The split control of the legislature since 1954 has been a source of anguished frustration for the Liberals and their supporters. Yet, whatever inefficiency or inaction may result, Minnesotans in general apparently have a marked preference for such diffusion of power. They apparently want not only the customary check and balance of the executive, legislative, and judicial departments upon one another, but the check of house against senate and senate against house possible when each chamber of the legislature is dominated by a different caucus.

On June 9, 1957, the "Minnesota Poll" provided evidence on this point, when it reported responses to the following question: "In the 1957 session, the Conservative members were in control of the state senate, while the Liberal members were in control of the lower house. Do you think this kind of divided control is a good thing or a bad thing for the state?" Those indicating they thought it a good thing were more than twice as many as those who thought it a bad thing:

	Total	Men	Women
It's a good thing	45%	49%	40%
It's a bad thing	20	21	18
No difference	1	2	under 1
No opinion	34	28	42

This same Poll asked a further question: "Suppose one group were to win control of both branches of the legislature. Which would you prefer it to be — the Conservatives or the Liberals?" The rather heavy Conservative plurality of response, shown in the tabulation below, suggests that Minnesotans have a strong desire for "stability" or "safety," as represented by the Conservatives.

	Total	Men	Women
Prefer Conservatives	40%	42%	39%
Prefer Liberals	22	29	15
Qualified answer	1	1	1
No opinion	37	28	45

Contrasts in the caucuses

The Liberal and Conservative caucuses of the 1959 legislature showed some decided differences in the geographic distribution of their strength. The 1st Congressional District, comprising the southeastern corner of the state (which has voted for Republican congressmen since 1859 with only two exceptions, in 1887 and

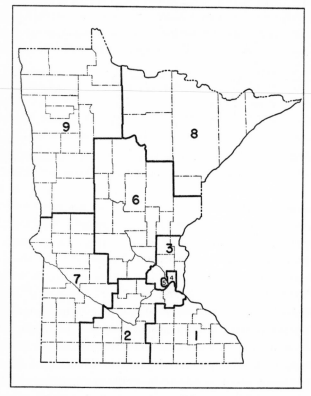

Figure 4. Congressional Districts (1960)

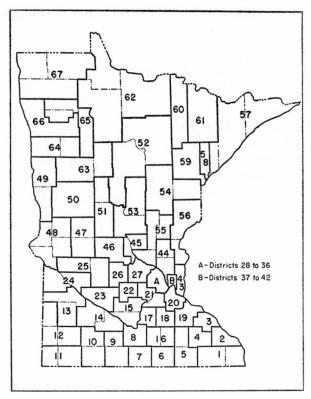

Figure 5. Legislative Districts (1960)

1891), sends 15 representatives to the state house, of whom 12, or 80 per cent, caucused with the Conservatives. Only one of its 9 senators caucused with the Liberals. In the adjoining 2nd District 12 out of 15 caucused with the Conservatives in the house and 8 out of 10 with that group in the senate. (The 14th legislative district cuts across the 2nd and 7th Congressional districts; its state senator was included here in the 2nd Congressional District.) Senators from the 7th District along the Dakota line divided 7 to 1 in favor of the Conservatives, although the house delegation of 20 was split 12 to 8 Liberal. Thus over half of the 43 Conservatives in the 1959 state senate and over half of the 59 Conservatives in the house came from the 1st, 2nd, and 7th Congressional districts which, though economically the agricultural backbone of the state, contain less than 30 per cent of Minnesota's population. (See Figures 4 and 5, which show present congressional and legislative districts.)

For the Liberals, the geographic centers of power were the three major metropolitan areas: Ramsey County (St. Paul), Hennepin County (Minneapolis), and St. Louis County (Duluth). Here live nearly 50 per cent of the state's population. Ten of the 12 house members from Ramsey, 12 of the 18 from Hennepin, and 12 of the 14 from St. Louis County and the rest of the 8th District caucused with the Liberals.

Tables 3 and 4 show interesting age and occupational contrasts.

Table 3. Age of Minnesota Legislators in the 1959 Session

Age	Senate				House			
	Conservatives		Liberals		Conservatives		Liberals	
	N	%	N	%	N	%	N	%
30 and under	0	0.0	4	16.6	1	1.6	4	5.2
31–40	3	7.0	3	12.5	12	20.4	23	32.6
41–50	6	14.0	8	33.3	13	22.2	17	23.5
51–60	21	48.8	7	29.2	16	27.1	13	18.0
61–70	13	30.2	1	4.2	16	27.1	14	19.4
71 and above	0	0.0	1	4.2	1	1.6	1	1.3

Table 4. Occupations of Minnesota Legislators in the 1959 Session

Occupation	Senate				House			
	Conservatives		Liberals		Conservatives		Liberals	
	N	%	N	%	N	%	N	%
Law	15	34.9	9	37.6	14	23.7	16	22.3
Farming	12	28.0	5	20.8	24	40.7	16	22.3
Business	9	20.9	2	8.3	11	18.6	11	15.3
Insurance and real estate	2	4.6	0	0.0	4	6.8	4	5.5
Teaching and school administration	1	2.3	2	8.3	0	0.0	2	2.8
Cooperatives	0	0.0	1	4.2	0	0.0	4	5.5
Journalism	3	7.0	0	0.0	0	0.0	5	6.9
Union official	0	0.0	0	0.0	0	0.0	5	6.9
Skilled laborer ...	0	0.0	2	8.3	0	0.0	2	2.8
Railroads	0	0.0	1	4.2	0	0.0	2	2.8
Banking	0	0.0	0	0.0	2	3.4	0	0.0
Other	1	2.3	2	8.3	4	6.8	5	6.9

There were no Conservative senators under 30, whereas the Liberals had four of their members in that age group. Twenty-one Conservative senators — nearly half of their total — fell between 51 and 60 years of age; Liberals had about one-third between 41 and 50 and less than one-third between 51 and 60. In the house likewise the Liberals were the more youthful party, with slightly more than twice as many members aged 40 or under. Although the average age on the house Rules Committee was 55, some of the committee chairmen of that chamber were extremely young — as, for example, the chairman of Appropriations, age 35; Taxes, 37; Motor Vehicles, 38; Judiciary, 35. In occupation, Conservatives drew a larger percentage of their members from business than did Liberals, but both groups also drew heavily on those with vocational backgrounds in law and farming.

The political parties and the caucuses

Minnesota legislators are elected without designation on the ballot of party membership or affiliation. For organizational purposes they group themselves into Conservative and Liberal caucuses — again without any explicit reference to party. A question often asked is how "partisan" is this nonpartisan body? One experienced political commentator, Ralph Fjelstad, after analyzing the voting during the 1953 session, was satisfied that Minnesota legislators tend to follow their factional commitments in much the same way that lawmakers in a partisan legislature respect their party lines. But are these legislators influenced by *party* lines as well as *caucus* lines?

The question cannot be answered simply, for the situation is a complex one. And it is not the same with respect to the two major parties.

Liberals in both legislative chambers have been frank to acknowledge their family ties with the Democratic-Farmer-Labor party. Four-fifths or more of the Liberals in the legislature openly identify themselves with the DFL; many of them have served as county or district committeemen. Moreover, the DFL constitution provides explicitly for representation from the Liberal caucuses on the party's state central and executive committees. As nonvoting members these caucus delegates attend the party's state conventions as well.

Such interrelationship of party and caucus has not always existed. During the Olson and Benson regimes important administrative proposals failed to become law because of faulty liaison and lack of cohesion, even during the two sessions of 1933 and 1937 when the house at least was nominally controlled by Liberals elected with Farmer-Laborite support. There were several reasons why the party, even in the days of its large popular majorities, lacked effective control of the legislature. In the first place, the Farmer-Laborites were unable to translate their heavy 1932 and 1936 majorities into senatorial strength because all members of the upper house are elected in "off years," not in presidential election years such as 1932 and 1936. Secondly, in the absence of party designation or pre-primary endorsement, voters were by no means sure of candidates' positions on major issues. A proof of this was the election of Conservative legislators from districts otherwise heavily Farmer-Laborite. The biographer of the Farmer-Labor party, Arthur Naftalin, has suggested a third reason: "During a reform era, in the absence of party discipline, the nonpartisanly elected legislator, left to his own judgment, finds Conservative affiliation an easier matter because it requires no positive avowal on his part in support of a definite program, whereas affiliation with the Liberals requires a rigorous understanding of, or at least sympathy for, a program of reform."

The Humphrey-Freeman organization resolved not to repeat the mistakes of the Farmer-Laborites. Accordingly, it gives the weight of party endorsement to approved candidates for the legislature, prints their names on its sample ballots, and sends its leaders into their districts to speak on their behalf. The DFL also has developed methods of recruiting new candidates; its precinct, ward, and county organizations are urged to interview liberally inclined farmers, businessmen, and professional men, to encourage their interest in politics, and to support them actively if they choose to run for legislative office. Organized labor groups and

Liberals already in the legislature have aided in these efforts, which since the early 1950's have brought considerable new talent into the Liberal caucuses, as for example Karl F. Grittner (who, after serving three terms in the house, was elected to the state senate in 1958), Joseph E. Karth (now United States representative from the 4th District, St. Paul), William L. Shovell (in 1959 chairman of the house Appropriations Committee), Peter S. Popovich (in 1959 chairman of the Motor Vehicles Committee), Donald D. Wozniak (in 1959 chairman of the house Tax Committee), and Donald Fraser (former law partner of Governor Freeman and an influential senate Liberal). The DFL believes that the recent increase in Liberal legislative strength is in no small measure due to its various promotional programs.

The relationship between the Republican party and the two Conservative caucuses is more complicated. While presently only about 40 per cent of the house Conservatives list themselves as active Republicans, some Conservative leaders in the house in recent years have held top-level positions in the party. Roy E. Dunn was national committeeman; John A. Hartle, speaker during three terms and long-time majority leader, was state chairman; P. Kenneth Peterson also served as state chairman while a member of the house. The list of Republican congressmen and state officials who served their political apprenticeship as Conservatives in the legislature is a long one, including in the recent period Ancher Nelsen, Odin Langen, George MacKinnon, and Albert H. Quie.

Among current senate Conservatives (28 per cent of whom acknowledge active participation in the Republican party), Donald O. Wright was a delegate to the 1940 Republican National Convention; Leo J. Lauerman was a Republican district chairman, as was Stanley W. Holmquist; Val Imm has held numerous party positions including membership on the state central committee; Walter J. Franz was treasurer of this important committee in 1954; Chris L. Erickson served as a county chairman; Fay G. Child worked as administrative assistant to Republican congressman Harold C. Hagen; and Robert R. Dunlap has been repeatedly mentioned along with former senator Elmer L. Andersen as a possible Republican candidate for governor.

Party workers among house Conservatives in the 1959 session included Harold R. Anderson (former state chairman of the Young Republican League), John Tracy Anderson (chairman of St. Paul's 12th Ward Club), Walter K. Klaus (chairman of the 2nd District), E. J. Windmiller (member of the state executive committee), and Clarence G. Langley (member of the state convention Platform Committee). Other representatives involved in Republican party organization at various levels are Roger F. Noreen, Clifton Parks, Rodney N. Searle, and F. Gordon Wright.

Despite this demonstrable interrelationship between party and caucus, a basic question remains: Do members of the nominally nonpartisan caucuses actually *vote* along party lines? In other words, are the caucuses in effect agents or representatives of their respective parties, regardless of what they are in theory?

Partial answers can be offered from an analysis of voting records on three proposals perennially advocated in the platforms of *both* major parties. The issues are these: a constitutional convention for the purpose of bringing the 1857 charter up to date (Table 5); party designation of state legislators (Table 6); and an "equal opportunities" or fair employment practices law (Table 7).

On all three issues the tables show that the Liberals conform more closely to the party position than do the Conservatives. Al-

Table 5. Roll Call Votes in the House (1949) and Senate (1955) on the Proposal to Call a Convention for Constitutional Revision*

Direction of Vote	House (1949)				Senate (1955)			
	Conservatives (N = 86)		Liberals (N = 44)		Conservatives (N = 48)		Liberals (N = 19)	
	N	%	N	%	N	%	N	%
Pro	46	54	34	77	11	23	16	84
Con	31	37	9	20	37	77	3	16

Source: Minnesota House, H.F. 810, April 8, 1949, p. 1889; Minnesota Senate, S.F. 23, March 15, 1955, p. 797.

*Because of absenteeism and nonvoting, percentages do not add to 100. There was in addition one house member listed as an "Independent" whose vote is not tabulated here.

Table 6. Roll Call Votes in the House (1951–1959) on Proposals to Establish Party Designation of State Legislators*

Session and Direction of Vote	Conservatives†		Liberals‡	
	N	%	N	%
1951 session				
Pro	28	32	25	60
Con	48	55	11	26
1953 session				
Pro	52	61	36	78
Con	28	33	8	17
1955 session				
Pro	19	29	43	65
Con	45	69	23	35
1957 session				
Pro	37	61	58	83
Con	21	34	11	16
1959 session				
Pro	9	15	52	72
Con	47	80	18	25

Source: Minnesota House, H.F. 9, February 13, 1951, pp. 406–7; H.F. 329, March 13, 1953, p. 1010; H.F. 12, February 15, 1955, p. 492; H.F. 41, February 15, 1957, pp. 446–47; H.F. 61, February 3, 1959, p. 15.

*Because of absenteeism and nonvoting, the percentages do not add to 100.

†The total number of Conservatives in 1951 was 88; in 1953, 85; in 1955, 65; in 1957, 61; in 1959, 59. (In 1951 one representative is listed as an "Independent.")

‡The total number of Liberals in 1951 was 42; in 1953, 46; in 1955, 66; in 1957, 70; in 1959, 72.

Table 7. Roll Call Votes in the House (1951–1955) on Proposals for a Fair Employment Practices Law*

Session and Direction of Vote	Conservatives†		Liberals‡	
	N	%	N	%
1951 session				
Pro	42	48	33	79
Con	43	49	5	12
1953 session				
Pro	41	48	40	87
Con	39	46	5	11
1955 session				
Pro	33	51	63	97
Con	28	43	2	3

Source: Minnesota House, H.F. 74, March 29, 1951, pp. 1520–21; H.F. 622, April 18, 1953, p. 2377; H.F. 778, April 7, 1955, pp. 1798–99.

*Because of absenteeism and nonvoting, the percentages do not add to 100.

†The total number of Conservatives in 1951 was 88; in 1953, 85; in 1955, 65. (In 1951 one representative is listed as an "Independent.")

‡The total number of Liberals in 1951 was 42; in 1953, 46; in 1955, 66.

though neither caucus achieved unanimity at any time, each showed a characteristic "center of gravity" suggestive of the tensions and alignments within it; and, on these issues at least, the independence of the Conservative caucus from the Republican party platform cannot easily be denied.

If we use the issue of reapportionment for legislative districts (also demanded by planks in both party platforms) as a further test case, the results are similar. During the ten years preceding the 1959 reapportionment law, numerous such bills were introduced in every session, few of which reached the roll-call stage. One that did reach a vote, the Bergerud-Gillen bill, passed the house in 1957, 68 to 61, with 64 per cent of the Conservatives and only 31 per cent of the Liberals opposing it. Some of the other reapportionment bills would have avoided cutting rural representation by increasing membership in one or the other of the chambers or by changing the basis of representation in one house to area instead of population. But the Bergerud-Gillen bill in essence directed the carrying out of the present constitutional mandate to reapportion on the basis of population. Of those in both caucuses voting against the measure, 83 per cent came from districts that are currently overrepresented in the legislature by approximately 20 per cent.

What all of this illustrates, some contend, is less the independence of the Conservative caucus from the Republican platform than the dependence of this caucus on its rural sources of power. This may well be true, for all four of the issues studied touch on rural-urban conflicts, and negative votes in all four instances reflect possible rural interests. For example, a new constitution might be resisted because it would presumably provide for reapportionment. Reapportionment itself would of course shift power to the metropolitan areas while taking away from rural Minnesota the overrepresentation it now enjoys. Even fair employment practices legislation becomes a sectional issue, for the rural economy depends in part on the use of seasonal labor in harvesting and canning.

The case against party designation

Certainly the influence of rural interests may be seen in the arguments advanced in support of the tradition of nonpartisanship in the legislature. Such veteran senators as Gordon Rosenmeier and Daniel S. Feidt argue vigorously that a Conservative (they prefer the label Independent) has no responsibility or accountability except that leading directly back to his own constituents. They assert that unlike Congress, a state legislature is concerned mainly with law enforcement, conservation, education, elections, local government, daylight saving time, liquor control, water safety, highway construction, teacher retirement plans, trucking permits, and many other issues on which public opinion is divided not primarily along party lines, but according to geographic — rural vs. urban — or economic interests. In representing his constituents' opinions, then, the legislator may well be forced into deviation from any and all party platforms.

The Independents conceive of a legislative caucus as a voluntary and perhaps temporary collaboration of like-minded persons for parliamentary purposes; by no means is this caucus to be construed as the arm, agent, or creature of a political party. Basically, the position of the supporters of nonpartisanship rests on their suspicion of, if not downright antagonism to, centralized party organizations, which they consider dominated by "bosses" and "machines." Implied here is belief in a disproportionate influence of metropolitan and labor interests on party councils. They fear too that gubernatorial domination of the legislature, as an outgrowth of "party discipline," would jeopardize the traditional separation of powers principle which has made American politics safe and cautious rather than efficient and over-hasty.

Another argument stems from the doctrine of legislative individuality and independence: to some Conservatives any party discipline smacks of a collectivism to which they are philosophically and temperamentally opposed. Their attitude is reminiscent of Edmund Burke's famous speech to his Bristol constituency affirming that "[a legislator's] unbiased opinion, his mature judgment, his enlightened conscience, he ought not to sacrifice to you,

72

to any man . . ." This is not to imply, however, that the Independents are unable or unwilling to act in concert or to form cabals to block legislation inimical to them.

Finally, the Independents maintain that public opinion in Minnesota backs them up, and that there is no majority sentiment in favor of party designation or any of the other devices of legislative partisanship. The results of a number of public opinion surveys conducted by the "Minnesota Poll" have generally confirmed this contention.

The Poll posed its questions on this subject in some such form as the following: "Some people think members of the state legislature in Minnesota should be elected under political party labels — that is, as Democrat-Farmer-Laborites or as Republicans — rather than on a no-party basis as they are now. Do you think legislators should be elected under party labels, or should not?" While sentiment for party designation increased threefold between 1945 and 1958, only once (in 1954) did a majority favor it:

Date	For Party Designation
March 1945	14%
February 1946	46
March 1947	39
July 1954	53
February 1955	38
April 1957	36
December 1958	40

It is interesting to note that this sentiment was in every instance less strong in the months following the legislative sessions than in the even-numbered years when the legislature does not ordinarily convene.

In some years the "Minnesota Poll" asked for party identification of the persons interviewed. Although party designation was slightly more popular among DFL interviewees than among Republicans, the difference never exceeded 4 per cent — perhaps a weaker response than might be expected in light of the official DFL position on party-caucus integration. Of the years tested only in 1946 (a period of Republican control of the state) was Republican sentiment for party designation stronger than that of the opposition; since then the GOP attitude seems to have cooled somewhat as the other party rose to power.

Arguments for party designation of the legislature

Despite the lack of strong popular support, a number of groups are currently agitating for a return to party designation of legislators — among them some important Republicans as well as spokesmen for the DFL; the Farmers Union; the League of Women Voters; and a number of labor unions.

They have various reasons for advocating party labels, but their arguments can be summarized as follows: (1) A party designated legislature would be better equipped to resist those special interests and local interests which now influence policy in a disproportionate and often undesirable manner. (2) A modern state government faces tremendous obligations in the fields of social, labor, and welfare legislation; to finance its new operations it must devise adequate but equitable taxation. On issues such as these, which affect all geographical areas and all economic groups, it is unrealistic to maintain that there can be no party position. On the contrary it is only the party system, representing as it does the broader coalitions of sectional and group interests, which can achieve social justice. (3) Reform platforms and proposals have little chance of enactment unless the governor can count on legislative support. The degree of executive-legislative teamwork necessary to implement election promises cannot be obtained without party designation. (4) The absence of party designation has in effect clothed with tremendous power a very small group of very conservative legislators elected from small constituencies or from districts where the voters know little about them. These men have been in a position to thwart Republican and Democratic governors elected by popular mandate, and their "invisible government" — so the argument runs — leads to cynical and irresponsible politics. In dealing with the issue of nonpartisanship in a study of the Minnesota legislature, Charles Adrian concluded that despite the imperfections of the American political party, "it is the best vehicle available for insuring responsibility of the law-maker to the people." (5) If legislators were elected with party labels, the precinct, ward, and county organizations would be re-vitalized and their work made more meaningful. There would be more interest in recruiting and supporting candidates, and in-creased participation in primary and general elections would re-sult.

Some basic governmental and political issues, pending and future

The issue of party designation is but one of the problems that face legislators in Minnesota. Indeed the legislature seems des-tined to figure prominently in most of the current or future "great debates" confronting the people of the state.

One of the most vital and controversial of these is constitution-al revision. Should the legislature now call a constitutional con-vention to revise or rewrite Minnesota's century-old basic charter, or should the lawmakers continue to rely on piecemeal amend-ment? Those who favor the convention method argue that be-cause of their complexity and their interdependence with existing articles, many reforms can be effected only through a revision of the entire constitution. Among the reforms mentioned frequently are these: a provision for the initiative and referendum, and for the short ballot for state executive officers (with its consequent expansion of gubernatorial appointive powers), the unfreezing of dedicated funds, the creation of mandatory reapportionment ma-chinery, the scheduling of annual instead of biennial legislative sessions, the elimination of obsolete language in the 1857 consti-tution (as for example that covering the suffrage and the election of United States senators), and the liberalizing of the present and unrealistic state debt limit of $250,000. It seems to many cheaper, more democratic, and more efficient to deal with such problems all at once in a convention dedicated to that task, rather than to work for the passage of separate amendments, some of which would necessarily be drafted in haste, insufficiently debated, and inadequately presented to the public.

Opponents of the convention method emphasize the greater safety and practicality of the piecemeal approach. They point, too, to the important reforms already achieved by various amendments. During the last ten years alone, entire articles have been rewritten covering such subjects as highways, judiciary, local governments, term of office for the chief executive officers (increased to four years beginning in 1962), and succession to the governorship in case of death or incapacity. It is admitted, of course, that amendments, particularly those of a more complicated or technical nature, have suffered a high mortality rate at the hands of Minnesota voters, and that the stiff requirement for passage (a majority of all votes cast at that election rather than a mere majority of those voting on the question) makes ratification difficult. However, the rejection rate has decreased significantly during the last ten years. In the period 1948–58, one out of every two amendments submitted to the voters won public approval at the polls, whereas 67.5 per cent of the amendments submitted between 1898 and 1946 failed to pass. No doubt the pressures for reform stemming from population increase and from postwar socioeconomic conditions helped to expose some of the inadequacies of the existing constitution; perhaps the "threat" of a constitutional convention, should the habitual rejection of amendments frustrate necessary reforms, also served as a stimulus. (See pp. 123–26 below.)

A second important issue is taxation — an area of legislative activity bristling with problems, as has already been indicated. Who should pay, and how much? Upon what kinds of property or economic activity should the major burden of state and local taxation rest? Should Minnesota incorporate a withholding plan into its income tax system? Should the state adopt a general sales tax, and if so, with what exemptions? Should such a tax be conceived as a replacement for other sources of revenue or as a supplement to these? Should personal property taxes on household goods or on farm and business inventories be reduced or eliminated? How can tax assessment and tax equalization procedures be reformed? How can citizens of the state be guaranteed a more equitable distribution of tax funds so that there will be proper and adequate revenue sources for local units as well as for the state government, with its ever-increasing needs? How does Minnesota's tax climate compare with that of competing states? Can the iron-ore companies absorb additional taxes? How can business and industry be attracted, retained, and encouraged to expand while at the same time required to pay their fair share of the tax burden?

Legislative reorganization and reform is of course of particular concern to the legislators. Should the number of committees be reduced, to permit the harassed lawmaker to devote more time to major issues? Should more formal and detailed journals and records be kept of legislative and committee proceedings? (This could affect future campaigns, by making possible a more explicit comparison of a candidate's promises with his post-election actions.) Should new rules be adopted to facilitate the return to the floor of bills pigeonholed or buried in hostile committees? Should the minority caucus be given the right to name its own representatives to legislative committees? Should legislator-attorneys be prohibited from representing private clients before state executive or regulatory agencies during the period between sessions? To what extent should lobbies be regulated? Should the legislature be freed from its present fiscal strait jacket, so that it might exercise greater power over all the revenues of the state?

There are a number of current problems relating to the executive branch. Should the governor be granted wide appointive powers similar to those enjoyed by the president of the United States? These new powers might enable the state chief executive to choose (with the advice and consent of the senate) such officials as the secretary of state, the treasurer, and perhaps even the attorney general, thereby building a strong and integrated cabinet to replace the present slate of constitutional officers each individually responsible to the electorate. Should the office of state auditor be re-defined as that of legislative watchdog over executive expenditures (by analogy with the United States comptroller general)? Should the Railroad and Warehouse Commission become a gubernatorially appointed rather than a popularly elected body? Or should the members of this commission be designated by the legislature, as is the present procedure with regard to the University of Minnesota's Board of Regents? To what extent should the governor be permitted to consolidate into a few major departments (Commerce, Law Enforcement, Revenue, etc.) the many functions now performed by a plethora of separate agencies, bureaus, commissions, boards, and divisions? How could the lines of authority and accountability in the state's central administration be clarified and strengthened? Would executive reorganization unduly strengthen the governorship, thereby jeopardizing the separation of power doctrine? Would executive consolidation together with the shortened ballot injure political parties who depend on a large slate of offices to evoke public interest and to permit compromise and coalition among their internal factions?

A challenge of intensifying concern to the legislature is that of metropolitan population increase, particularly in and around the Twin Cities. The Metropolitan Planning Commission established by the 1957 legislature to provide "advisory metropolitan planning service for the area consisting of Anoka, Dakota, Hennepin, Ramsey, and Washington counties" (Carver and Scott counties joined later) has submitted estimates of great significance to both state and local governments. By 1980, according to the commission's figures, this metropolitan area alone will be obliged to provide for 600,000 more residents, for 250,000 more jobs, for 175,000 more dwelling units, for 140 more schools, for 900 new miles of streets and highways, for a 120-million-gallon daily increase in water consumption, and for 700 more policemen and firemen. The enormous financial burdens and other problems of "megalopolitan" growth may force the legislature into new statutory as well as merely advisory roles, especially as these new population concentrations affect the tax base, the pattern of revenue expenditures, the balance of rural as against urban interests, and other statewide issues.

One specific problem connected with metropolitan growth can be expected to evoke a vigorous legislative battle. Since the population growth of Minnesota as a whole is not keeping pace with that in some other states, it will probably lose one of its nine congressional seats after the 1960 census. The legislature will then have to redraw district boundaries. And it will have to take account of the population shifts that have made the present districts very unequal. For example, in the 1956 congressional race the combined Republican-DFL vote in the 9th District was 111,-853. In the same election 245,072 votes, or more than double the 9th District total, were cast in the 3rd District, which covers parts of Minneapolis and its suburbs. Moreover, present population estimates indicate a growing disparity. Almost all the counties in Districts 7 and 9 show a rate of growth below the state average, and a good many had a net loss in population between 1950 and 1958. Hennepin (3rd and 5th districts), Stearns (6th District), and Dakota (2nd District) are metropolitan or semi-urban counties with population increases well above the state average. These are the areas that will be particularly affected by redistricting.

There are many other issues that will also come before the legislature. But these indicate the scope and complexity of legislative business in the future.

4

LOBBIES BEFORE THE LEGISLATURE

The how and why of lobbies

MOST people are confused, if not downright misinformed, about the role of lobbies in a democratic society. The subject is an especially pertinent one for Minnesotans, since their state's very powerful non-party-designated legislature may well attract more than its share of lobbyists.

Lobbies are not unique to the democratic form of government, but are better detected and studied in such an environment. In an authoritarian context the same pressures are exerted in a carefully concealed, mysterious, subterranean fashion. In the United States, on the other hand, lobbying is part and parcel of our political tradition. By inference it is sanctioned in the first amendment to the Constitution, which safeguards "the right of peaceful assembly and of petition for redress of grievances"; Article I of the Minnesota constitution declares that "Government is instituted for the security, benefit and protection of the people, in whom all political power is inherent, together with the right to alter, modify or reform such government, whenever the public good may require it."

A lobby may be defined as an interest group concerned primarily with the promotion or modification of, or opposition to, legislation and governmental regulations. As such, its activities may impinge on the legislature, on committees and individual members thereof, or on the executive branch together with its bureaus and agencies, or on regulatory commissions charged with the application to particular cases of extant but broadly stated laws — indeed, at various times, on all of these.

A lobby is born out of the specialized, homogeneous needs of a particular occupational or social group. Doctors, lawyers, farmers, teachers, businessmen, bankers, and working people in general usually lack the time or the know-how to keep the legislative process under constant scrutiny or to influence it toward their group's advantage. Consequently such people may found associations to represent them on Capitol Hill and express their wishes. These associations — call them "lobbies" if you will — may employ full-time or part-time staffs, may operate continuously or *ad hoc*, may actually vote some of their own membership into political office. (As one magazine writer put it, referring somewhat wistfully to the Minnesota situation, "You don't need lobbyists here; this legislature has its own built-in lobby.") Though they usually exert direct pressure on the legislature and other policy-making bodies, some lobbies pursue their objectives more indirectly by working on the home constituency of a senator or representative. This is often very effective just before a primary or general election.

Like the Constitution itself, lobbies can be termed "party blind." They work within, between, and across party and caucus lines. With a more deeply committed membership, better financing, and clearer goals, they are frequently more than a match for a much larger but much more heterogeneous political party.

Good and bad lobbies

Lobbies have been praised and condemned, investigated and restricted. They have been called "the third house of the legislature" and blamed for immoral pressures and undercover operations. The federal government and thirty-eight of the states (though not Minnesota) require lobbyists to register, indicating their employers and their objectives; in some states, they must also file financial reports.

In their defense it can be argued that lobbies supply lawmakers with necessary information, that they serve to check and balance each other, that they enunciate the legitimate objectives of particular professional or socioeconomic groupings, and that with their specialized backgrounds they can assess the beneficial or deleterious effects of proposed laws and regulations. However, nobody will claim that lobbying is an unmixed blessing. Lobbyists sometimes speak only for themselves and the bureaucratic officialdom of their organization rather than for the rank-and-file membership, whose only function is to watch apathetically from the sidelines. In a larger sense lobbying may be injurious to a society, for wherever lobbying is rampant the unorganized and inarticulate interests (as for example the long-suffering consumer) are especially apt to be ignored.

Then there is the question of lobbying tactics. Many of these are legitimate, useful, and ingenious. Some — such as threats, bribes, and "deals" — are explicitly illegal and punishable. Other lobby strategies are in the border areas of political morality: it is one thing to persuade a legislator with facts and reasons, and quite another to assail him with distorted statistics, juggled graphs, exaggerated propaganda, and deliberate misinformation. Those who defend lobbying point out that the meretricious claims of one pressure group are likely to be refuted by its competitors, and that a free-for-all on Capitol Hill is evidence of a healthy body politic. With each lobby claiming that what is good for it is good for all, democratic theory presumes the emergence of a majority consensus on what is actually in the interest of all the people. Those holding this somewhat overoptimistic view argue that if all interests, organized and unorganized, are allowed to interact openly and freely, more justice than injustice will prevail in the end.

Lobbying, then — its functions, merits, abuses — is a controversial and complicated issue best studied in terms of particular cases. Out of the literally hundreds of groups and associations which converge on the state capitol during each legislative session, six have been selected for a closer look. These six organizations, of course, perform many services in addition to lobbying — educational, economic, social — but for the purposes of this chapter they will be studied chiefly in terms of their impact on the legislature.

LOBBIES BEFORE THE LEGISLATURE

The Minnesota League of Women Voters

Established in 1920, the Minnesota League of Women Voters is a powerful civic reform group with approximately 5,500 members distributed throughout the state but heavily concentrated in St. Paul, Minneapolis, and Duluth. According to its own publications, "the League is nonpartisan. It takes action in support of or in opposition to selected governmental issues, but it does not support or oppose . . . candidates . . . or . . . political parties." It urges its members to work in the party of their choice and to support issues and candidates conducive to good government on the local, state, and national levels. League programs have included campaigns to get out the vote, meetings with candidates, legislative workshops, and election campaign schools. Among League publications (most of the pamphlets designed for study and discussion groups) are *You Are the Government* (1949, 1958), *Reapportionment in Minnesota: Democracy Denied* (1954), *The State You're In* (1958), *St. Paul at Your Service* (1955), *Minneapolis Is Your Business, ABC's of City Government* (1955), and *Ninety Days of Lawmaking* (1939).

The League has advocated legislation for aid to dependent women and children, for low-income housing, for public health improvements, for fair employment practices, for an increase in the minimum school year, for compulsory school attendance, for teacher tenure safeguards and teacher retirement funds, and for school reorganization. Particularly interested in structural and constitutional reforms, the Minnesota League has been a constant and patient supporter of constitutional revision, party designation for legislators, legislative reapportionment, registration of lobbyists, election law recodification, and civil service. Throughout its existence it has also campaigned for international cooperation and for support of the League of Nations and the United Nations.

Organizationally the Minnesota League operates on local, state, and (as a member of the National League of Women Voters) national levels. Its members may meet, study, and "act" in small discussion units; they may also participate in local, area, and statewide annual assemblies and conventions. The governing power at the state and national levels resides in elective boards of directors who during their term of office are forbidden to engage in political party work. Local units must approve issues selected for study and for support. Use of study materials and handbooks and recourse to expert consultants are encouraged in all phases of the programming.

Preparatory to a legislative session the League may ask lawmakers where they stand on such issues as party designation and reapportionment. After the session opens the state office issues "Legislative Reports" giving committee appointments, times and places of committee meetings, and schedules of important hearings. League members are encouraged to attend and in some instances to testify; few are the days when members of the League cannot be seen attending committee hearings or "speaking to their representatives." Cartoons showing them (in outlandish hats) buttonholing some frightened legislator have been a not-infrequent feature of the state press.

"Legislative Bulletins" and "Capitol Letters" provide additional information, as for example important committee votes not recorded in the press and testimony pertinent to League-supported issues. In "After Action" reports measures in which the League is interested are traced from their introduction through all the stages of committee hearings, floor battles, and votes. These case histories explain successes and failures, single out the positive or negative contributions of legislators, analyze proponents' and opponents' speeches, and probe into parliamentary delaying tactics.

Cartoons and jokes about "women in politics" notwithstanding, no one can deny the sincere, intelligent, and professional approach of League workers. Supporters acclaim the perennial championing by the League of neglected, unspectacular, and vital issues involving technical and structural reforms. Whereas capitol corridors teem with people who want something for themselves at their neighbor's expense, the genius of the League lies in its disinterestedness and in the emphasis it puts on basic questions of political philosophy.

The strengths of the League become its weaknesses when seen from another point of view. Its detractors read the prejudices of the well-educated and the well-to-do into League activities and accuse it of failing in representativeness. Working girls might well be uncomfortable in a League study session where the atmosphere and vocabulary resemble those of a meeting of the American Association of University Women. Conservatives look askance at the League's fondness for fair employment practices, public housing, and related social welfare measures. In such quarters its preoccupation with constitutional revision and legislative reapportionment is interpreted as an "egghead" tinkering with the *status quo*, and it is associated in some minds with urban pressure groups or with the policies of labor unions. Some candidates upon receiving League questionnaires before an election complain that such queries represent an invasion of their privacy and a threat to their independence — but such criticism may redound more to the candidate's discredit than the League's.

League friends and critics alike concede without much debate that League members are well-informed and persevering, that their legislative spokesmen are highly competent, that they are not afraid to fight for what they consider right.

The Minnesota Employers' Association

"We believe that what helps business helps the people who work for business. . . . that what hurts business hurts the people who work for business. We believe wholeheartedly in the free enterprise system which built Minnesota and America." Thus runs a memorandum from the Minnesota Employers' Association to all Minnesota legislators. Nationally affiliated with various other business and industrial councils, the Minnesota association comprises approximately 1,700 employers. It was founded in 1908 to help create a favorable legislative climate for business. Membership is open to all employers of nine or more and the dues are computed on the basis of fifty cents for every $1,000 of annual payroll subject to the state's unemployment compensation tax, but with a minimum of $25 and a maximum of $750.

The association has a 32-member Board of Directors who meet at least annually, but the real legislative work is done by Otto F. Christianson, its executive vice president, and Julius E. Kubier, its executive assistant. Mr. Christianson, the chief spokesman for the organization, has delivered hundreds of speeches to civic, business, professional, and fraternal groups throughout the state. During the sessions he testifies before legislative committees, supplying research materials that support the case for employers and presenting arguments in favor of economy and stability in government. More informally he seeks to create legislative good-will through luncheons and social occasions to which lawmakers are invited. Meanwhile association members are kept informed of events on the Hill by means of regular "Legislative Reports," printed in the association bulletin *Guidepost.*

These reports list committee members, analyze bills affecting employers' interests, and discuss the tactics of the opposition forces. At the beginning of the 1959 session, for example, the board unanimously condemned the governor's budget message which "although proposing millions for relief and welfare . . . suggested nothing for increasing employment . . . Apparently the Governor has thrown his lot with those who hold little hope for the future of business and industry in our state . . . such as encouraging business to come to or expand in Minnesota. In fact he offers industry ample incentive to expand elsewhere or to leave the state." Reports in subsequent issues of the *Guidepost* reveal the type of legislation opposed by the association: temporary disability insurance, upward revision of the unemployment compensation rates, equal pay for equal work done by women.

Friends and enemies will agree that the Minnesota Employers' Association gives its clients their money's worth. "The MEA can look upon the 1953 session of the Minnesota legislature," political reporter Fred Neumeier wrote in the *St. Paul Pioneer Press* in May 1953, "as a success. Not one bill opposed by the association became law. The recommendations . . . on workmen's compensation and unemployment compensation were adopted. The association fought labor bosses to a standstill on their efforts to toss out state laws restricting the activities of unions." Among the measures opposed was the fair employment practices or employment on merit measure. Though less successful in 1955 and 1957 in blocking this and other labor-supported laws, the association during the 1959 session assisted in defeating bills that would have increased workmen's and unemployment compensation benefits and would have broadened their coverage to include employees of charitable hospitals. An index of the association's strength might be found in a few statistics on some of the important measures it "watched" during the 1959 session. Of 53 labor measures introduced in the house (43 of which were Liberal-sponsored) all but 2 were killed either in that chamber or in the senate; of 26 unemployment compensation bills (24 of which had Liberal backing) only 4 survived; and of the 25 measures on workmen's compensation (the Liberals introduced 21), 20 failed.

On the Hill, Otto Christianson is known as an extremely well-informed and tireless lobbyist. Fundamentally conservative, he has vehemently opposed all those measures commonly associated with the welfare state, has fought against constitutional revision and party designation, and has condemned anything that might reinforce the power of organized labor. He keeps a wary eye on governmental budgets and appropriations and is quick to expose what he considers unnecessary expenditures imposing new burdens on already hard-pressed taxpayers. To the Liberals he has often appeared to be the very symbol of business reaction, blindly opposing the broadening base of social and economic power and resisting the claims of human values over profits and property.

The Minnesota AFL-CIO Federation of Labor

Although some union activity goes back to the early 1830's, large-scale organization of American labor had to wait until the post-Civil War decades. Hard times in the 1870's accelerated unionization and brought on strikes. In Minnesota, the St. Paul Trades and Labor Assembly was founded in 1882, the Minneapolis Trades Assembly one year later, and the Minnesota State

Federation of Labor in 1890. From the beginning the question of political activity by unions loomed large, and after a bitter battle among Socialists, Progressives, and others included in its membership, the Federation of Labor added a clause to its constitution in 1896 to the effect that "Party politics, whether they be Democratic, Republican, Socialist, Populistic, or Prohibition, or any other, shall have no place in the conventions of this Federation, nor shall the delegates of any political party be admitted."

Yet legislative issues, especially when conceived narrowly in terms of wages, hours, and living conditions, involved the Federation of Labor throughout its existence with politics and politicians. Generally although by no means uniformly inclined toward the Farmer-Labor party and the DFL, the Minnesota State Federation found it expedient to develop an effective working relationship with the long line of Republican governors and the Conservative leaders of the Minnesota legislature. There were even instances of Federation of Labor endorsement of Republicans in congressional elections on the principle of "rewarding friends and punishing enemies."

An indication of the current political potential of organized labor in Minnesota is to be found in its sheer weight of numbers; since the AFL-CIO merger in 1956, the combined strength of organized labor (including the various railroad brotherhoods and other independent union movements) has been approximately 160,000 members.

In addition to its immediate concern with labor problems per se, the Minnesota labor movement has given past or present support to many general reforms, such as provision of free textbooks for school children, abolition of the convict contract system, strengthening of education on the elementary, secondary, vocational, and adult levels, state governmental reorganization, initiative, referendum, and recall, income taxation, veterans' benefits, party designation, constitutional revision, legislative reapportionment, state civil service, fair employment practices, and income tax withholding. Its overriding concern during the 1930's was of course the issue of relief and unemployment compensation for the jobless and hungry. Led by such men as E. G. Hall, Robert A. Olson (Federation of Labor president since 1938), George A. Lawson (Federation of Labor secretary, 1914–54), and Robert Hess (former state CIO president), Minnesota labor has fought against anti-secondary-boycott laws, union suability, "right to work" laws, no-strike laws for public employees, and general sales taxes.

Structurally, the Federation of Labor is governed by its biennial conventions and its special conferences. Between conventions decisions on legislative questions are made by an executive committee presently headed by President Olson, Executive Vice President Hess, and Secretary General Neil C. Sherburne. This committee includes twenty-three other vice presidents representing important union groupings. Committees on legal problems, research, public relations, and political education are responsible to the executive committee, which in turn is responsible to the 1,300-delegate convention, attended by representatives from 600 local unions, 38 local departments (building, metals, etc.), and 26 city central bodies (trades and labor assemblies). Membership dues for the affiliated local unions are based on a per capita tax of eleven cents per member per month, according to present rates. There is a fee of $1 per year per convention delegate from each city central body and $2 from each affiliated organization.

Much of the lobbying done by the Minnesota labor movement has been the work of its executive leaders, such men as Robert Olson, Robert Hess, Frank Starkey, and William D. Gunn, and of the representatives of the various railroad brotherhoods, as for example L. J. Covey, the chairman and legislative representative of the Brotherhood of Railroad Trainmen. Research staffs provide background data on the thirty to fifty measures sponsored or supported by the labor movement in each session, and they offer help to friendly legislators in search of ammunition to counteract the lobbying efforts of business, taxpayer, and other groups hostile to labor objectives. Union publications keep tab on lawmakers and biennial legislative reports give "box scores" on individual voting records which reveal "favorable" and "unfavorable" totals as measured by labor criteria, together with brief discussions of parliamentary successes, failures, and obstacles. Labor leaders have found this material useful in keeping campaigns centered on issues and in educating union members about the causes for which labor fights.

For either tactical or ideological reasons the Federation of Labor was for many years much more reluctant than the younger CIO to join forces with New Dealers and Fair Dealers; more recently Minnesota labor has cooperated more openly with other liberal groups, has broadened its interests to include more general social and humanitarian goals, and has sought *rapprochement* with certain state farm and cooperative organizations.

Its influence within DFL councils and its effective support of friendly legislators have given the labor movement considerable legislative leverage. This was particularly true in the 1955 and 1957 sessions.

As with any other pressure group, an evaluation depends on one's own point of view. Critics evince considerable alarm at the burgeoning power of organized labor within the DFL and the Liberal caucus of the house. Conservative opposition to party designation, constitutional revision, and the other Liberal issues which labor supports may help to explain the old-guard position on the political activities of labor. For their part, labor leaders insist that their power has been grossly exaggerated. They complain of being used as whipping boys by conservative interests who seek to isolate them from their rank and file and who seek to isolate the labor movement as a whole from the farmers by exploiting charges of labor racketeering and bossism. The broad modern objectives of labor, union leaders assert, are coincident with rather than inimical to the general welfare. They say that they fight an uphill battle at best in a state where disproportionate representation prevents genuine majority rule and where the opposition enjoys a near-monopoly of the means of communication.

The Minnesota Farm Bureau Federation

Since its founding in 1919 the Minnesota Farm Bureau Federation has grown to include some 30,000 farm families. Affiliated with the American Farm Bureau Federation and its 1.5 million families, the Minnesota group is a "free, independent, non-governmental, voluntary organization of farm and ranch families . . . to achieve educational improvement, economic opportunity, and social advancement." It further defines itself as "local, national and international in . . . scope and influence, and non-partisan, non-sectarian, and non-secret in character." It claims to speak for all kinds of farmers and to be the true "Voice of Organized Agriculture," and it insists that the leaders and the voting members of the organization must be farmers.

The organizational philosophy of the Farm Bureau places sovereignty at the grassroots. The county is the basic unit of the organization, and policies are passed on to the state level only after receiving majority approval at the lower level. In state conventions voting strength is based on county membership, each county being allotted at least one vote plus additional votes where membership exceeds 600. State board members are elected at these annual conventions, as well as an executive board which carries out policies approved by convention resolutions. The headquarters staff includes an executive secretary, five field representatives, and additional personnel engaged in research, public relations, and legislative contacts.

The general position taken by the Minnesota Farm Bureau Federation can be gauged by listing some of the main themes of the resolutions ratified during its convention in November 1958. It registered opposition to party designation of legislators; it favored a constitutional amendment guaranteeing at least one representative to the legislature per county, with reapportionment to be based on area as well as population; it disapproved of a constitutional convention, asserting that the amendment process would permit necessary revisions; it vigorously opposed daylight saving time; it championed state college expansion in the towns of Crookston and Morris; it rejected additional basic aids to schools; it objected to further centralization "in the field of higher education"; and it deplored "any attempt to force consolidation of rural, village or city schools by legislation without approval of the majority vote of the district concerned." In regard to labor legislation, it favored a "right to work" law and urged that unions be placed under the antitrust laws. It opposed the extension of benefit periods for unemployment compensation and it wanted neither minimum wages for farm employees nor "any increase in industrial minimum wages." Actions "taken by labor unions to strike when agricultural products are moving to market" came under its censure.

The federation proposed that the names of beneficiaries of public assistance be published monthly. It opposed income tax withholding plans, gasoline tax increases, and iron-ore tax increases, but accepted a sales tax if agriculture did not have to "bear an unfair burden" and if such a tax was a replacement for other taxes. It favored retention of the township assessor system and opposed any increase in state levies on real and personal property — fields it believed should be reserved for city, county, and local revenues. It regarded itself as the sponsor or steady friend of marketing and bargaining associations like the Central Livestock Association, the Land O'Lakes Cooperative Marketing Association, the Twin Cities Milk Producers Association, and the Midwest Wool Growers Marketing Association, and as a contributor to the beginnings of the Blue Cross–Blue Shield health insurance programs.

Geographically, Minnesota Farm Bureau strength is concentrated in the 1st and 2nd Congressional districts, which include Minnesota's "deep south" counties of Blue Earth, Mower, Fillmore, Martin, Freeborn, and Cottonwood. Scott, Dakota, and McLeod counties a little to the north are also Farm Bureau bas-

Table 8. Comparison of Minnesota Farm Bureau Strength and Conservative-Liberal Representation in the Legislature

No. of Bureau Members per Legislative District	Conservatives	Liberals	Conservative Advantage
900 and over	21	5	16
700–899	19	11	8
500–699	9	2	7
300–499	21	16	5
100–299	15	14	1

tions, as are parts of the 9th Congressional District — in particular Kittson and Polk counties. In the 6th District Meeker and Stearns counties have heavy membership in the organization.

Table 8 shows a rather definite concurrence between Conservative representation in the legislature and Farm Bureau strength. Since many other factors are involved (as for example land values, and the personalities of individual candidates) it would be absurd to impute a cause-and-effect relationship to these figures; nevertheless the potent influence of the Farm Bureau Federation on the Minnesota legislature is beyond question.

What is involved here is something more than mere lobbying. Granted that the Farm Bureau gives dinners for legislators and provides them with research materials and talks with them personally through Executive Secretary Dale Nelson and President C. W. Myers, it still seems likely that the organization's program succeeds chiefly because so many legislators are themselves farmers. If not actually tilling the soil, many of them are engaged in occupations so closely interwoven with farming (banking, real estate, small town businesses, small town legal practices, weekly newspapers) that their thinking and voting may be rather naturally in harmony with the thinking of the Farm Bureau leadership.

This raises again the question of how democratic and inclusive the organization in fact is. Its opponents suspect it of being led by and for the upper-income farmer, the corporation farmer, farm-connected industries, and even chambers of commerce. Some consider that despite its local foundations it is dominated by a bureaucracy that imposes its views or those of the national organization on the individual members. Organized labor has little cause for friendship with the Farm Bureau, which has always opposed union growth and has favored government economy at the expense of welfare legislation. Proponents of political reforms (such as an overhaul and centralization of state administration, reapportionment, and reduction of the number of elective offices) feel that the conservative resistance of the federation has had much to do with their legislative defeats.

Spokesmen for the Minnesota Farm Bureau counter these arguments with some of their own. Theirs is a farmers' organization, they explain, which opposes urban pressures and big government and socialism on principle, but it is not supine or uncreative. The federation claims credit for better roads, for genuine farm cooperatives, for reduced marketing costs, for a brucellosis control program, for crop research, for sponsoring rural electrification. Consistent with its own minimized-government doctrines, it has remained hostile to government aid for farmers whether through production payment plans, acreage reductions, or high and rigid price supports. In the federation's own words, "the future of farming depends on its being a free [and] competitive enterprise . . . regulated by supply and demand and with as few regulations as necessary."

The Minnesota Farmers Union

Unlike the rival Farm Bureau Federation, the Minnesota Farmers Union (in operation by 1930) has never been known for conservative inclinations. Strongly tied to the politics of protest, dissent, and Populism, the Farmers Union has been extremely critical of various aspects of capitalism, particularly of the profit and credit mechanism. Throughout its existence it has prided itself on speaking for the "little fellow" and the "real dirt farmer."

The base of its organizational pyramid is its claimed membership of over 40,000 families. Each chartered county union elects a president; these county presidents compose a state board of directors and elect from their members biennially an executive committee of five members, one of whom serves as state president. Policies are formulated at the annual conventions in which each local unit wields voting strength in proportion to its membership.

"The family-type farm is the keystone of our policy," according to the preamble of a 1959 Farmers Union publication. In the interests of protecting and improving the status of the family farm the Farmers Union has not hesitated to call upon the state or federal government for action and intervention. It approves of state income tax withholding, increases in iron-ore taxes, low-cost public power, and the establishment of a public service commission to "regulate light and power rates and safeguard municipal power systems or REA cooperatives from pirating or other unfair competition tactics by private power firms." In its plan for legislative reapportionment, one house would be based on population and the other "largely or entirely" on area. Its attitudes toward labor differ markedly from those of the Farm Bureau. "Farmers should recognize," the Farmers Union states, "that the so-called 'right-to-work' laws are not designed to protect the workers, but rather to undermine the system of collective bargaining which organized labor has developed over a period of years." Members are urged to do business with the Farmers Union Grain Terminal Association, the Farmers Union Central Exchange, and Farmers Union Insurance.

There is strong opposition to a state retail sales tax in the organization, and it asks for tax relief for "farmers, small businessmen and wage earners." It would like to see the elimination of the personal property tax on "farm livestock, and crop inventories, including inventories of farm-stored grain." It has a program of educational aims, including strengthening of the University of Minnesota branch system, federal aid for construction of schools, and "expanded state aid for support of public schools"; and it recommends "a study of the principles and practices of cooperatives . . . in the course of study of our colleges and high schools." In a strongly anti-Benson vein it has sought mandatory price support payments at 100 per cent of parity for both storable and perishable farm commodities. The Farmers Union wants party designation for legislators and proposes that "legislative assignments and committee posts [be given] on basis of competence and knowledge rather than simply on seniority."

The community of interests between farmer and laborer has become a basic tenet of the Farmers Union. In bringing together organized labor and the cooperative movement it hopes to generate legislative power to convert its objectives (many of which are labor's as well) into laws, regulations, and state-sponsored services.

Representing the Minnesota Farmers Union at the legislature and working closely with M. W. Thatcher, the general manager of the Grain Terminal Association, are the organization's long-time president, Edwin Christianson, and the executive secretary, Clinton W. Hess. In its weekly newsletters and bimonthly newspapers the Farmers Union makes no secret of its generally strong support of the DFL, the Liberal caucus, and the Freeman administration. Its party proclivities are also indicated by the numerous speaking appearances of Senator Humphrey and various DFL congressmen at conventions and banquets of the Farmers Union, the Grain Terminal Association, and the Central Exchange. In rural counties many of the DFL precinct workers are active in the farm and elevator cooperatives. Some interrelationship between degree of strength of the Minnesota Farmers Union and Conservative loss of power might be inferred from Table 9 — though here again multiple factors make it hazardous to assume a cause-and-effect relationship.

Table 9. Comparison of Farmers Union Strength and Liberal-Conservative Representation in Legislature

No. of Farmers Union Member Families per Legislative District	Liberals	Conservative	Conservative Advantage
900 and over	22	27	5
700 to 899	5	16	11
500 to 699	18	33	15

Whereas the Minnesota Farm Bureau is entrenched in the southern counties, Farmers Union strength comes from central and western Minnesota and from the Red River Valley in particular.

Being so unlike the Farm Bureau, the Farmers Union has drawn the opposite brand of criticism. To the conservative, its "government-consciousness" smacks of socialism. Its cooperation with organized labor arouses in some rural quarters an instinctive suspicion of unions and union bosses. The leftist tendencies of some extremist Farmers Union leaders back in the 1930's further aggravated these antagonisms. Today's Farmers Union leaders, however, maintain that their organization is the one truly liberal force in agriculture, and that the family farm and the farmers' cooperative represent rural America's best bulwark against the ruthless and impersonal industrialization of modern agriculture.

The Minnesota Education Association

The Minnesota Education Association "makes no political commitments, recognizes no political alignments . . . and it seeks the good will and cooperation of all groups, confident that the education of the youth of Minnesota is a common interest — a common concern." As announced in its articles of incorporation, it proposes "to foster professional zeal, improve teaching, promote educational interests and advocate standards of education." Founded in 1861, it has a current membership of over 24,000 classroom teachers; principals, superintendents, and some faculty members from state and private colleges also belong.

Its more than 400 chartered and affiliated local chapters are grouped into Central, Minneapolis, Northeast, Northern, St. Paul, Southwest, and Western divisions. They send delegates at the ratio of one for each 200 members to the 155-member annual assembly. Final authority lies in a 19-member executive board, which appoints an executive secretary (for many years Walter E. Englund) to manage the day-by-day business at association headquarters: membership files, accounting, legislative contacts, field service, public relations, research, insurance, and publication of the *Minnesota Journal of Education.*

Like other interest groups the association considers it a major duty to inform its members about capitol affairs. Newsletters report on senate and house committee activities and discuss bills and proposals affecting school interests. For many years the periodical *Windows on Legislation* was edited by A. L. Almen, a twenty-year chairman of the senate Education Committee. To supplement its normal legislative contacts, the association headquarters issues special "calls for help" to the membership during times of crisis; the result is a barrage of letters to a legislator or a committee chairman. Perhaps this device is the most effective weapon in the organization's arsenal.

As might be expected, the association's legislative program pertains chiefly though not exclusively to schools, teachers, and school finance. For years it has opposed the diversion of permanent school funds to any purpose other than primary and secondary education. Its "platform" has included among other things (1) increased state aid to school districts; (2) state income tax withholding; (3) professional standards for county superintendents of schools; (4) teacher retirement programs; (5) increased state aid to junior colleges; (6) salary increases for the faculties of state colleges and for personnel on the State Board of Education; (7) statewide minimum salary scales for teachers; (8) standardization and equalization of tax assessment procedures; (9) liquidation of school districts which have been inoperative for two or more years.

The Minnesota Education Association has had considerable success in converting its objectives into state law. Among other things it has helped secure a statewide "fair dismissal" statute, repeated increases in state aids to local districts, a teacher retirement plan, recodification of education laws, and a teacher referendum on social security coverage. However, the 1959 legislature rejected driver education, elimination of closed school districts, a scholarship and loan program, and a $6 million appropriation for junior college expansion. All things considered, the association's capitol batting average is higher than that of most lobbies, partly because its well-educated, professionalized membership applies pressure in behalf of a cause to which the state, following frontier tradition, has already become deeply committed. Legislators who can turn a deaf ear to most blandishments are reluctant to "offend the teachers." Too, the organization has influential Conservative friends who will support appropriations for education despite their habitual unwillingness to spend any money on "less worthy" enterprises.

Not everybody looks with unqualified favor on the Minnesota Education Association. It has working agreements with the Minnesota School Board Association and it has sometimes lobbied jointly with that group. Some teachers find it altogether too hospitable toward the school administrator's point of view and claim that they were pressured into joining by principals or superintendents who prefer this organization to the Minnesota Federation of Teachers (AFL). For these and other reasons the Federation of Teachers detects a "company union" taint in the Minnesota Education Association and accuses it of reflecting "managerial interests" rather than the classroom teacher's. The association's stand on fiscal policy draws criticism from those who feel that if the state's permanent trust funds remain dedicated solely to education, as the association insists they should, the state may have to adopt a sales tax in order to meet its needs for ready revenue.

Some of the other lobbies

To paraphrase Gilbert and Sullivan, a legislator's lot is not a happy one. These six lobbies and many more demand attention from the lawmaker not only throughout the ninety-day session but intermittently during his full term as well.

Consider some of the other pressure groups competing for the legislator's support. The Minnesota Association for Mental Health has a coherent program backed by constant dissemination of facts and statistics. It claims that the state's excessive hospital readmission rates point to inadequate facilities, that psychiatric and other services are too heavily concentrated in the Twin Cities, that the state ought to finance increased research programs. The Minnesota Motor Transport Association, no weakling among lobbies, represents common and private carriers, petroleum carriers, household goods movers — most of the transport vehicles moving on rubber tires. It agitated through many sessions for the so-called fifty-foot truckers' bill — a measure opposed with equal vigor by the railroads and railroad brotherhoods. Add to these the Minnesota Taxpayers' Association, with its dedication to economy, its antagonism to income tax withholding, and its support of the sales tax. The Lake Superior Industrial Bureau is an organ through which the mining companies appeal for tax relief. Speaking through William Montague and Richard Hastings, it argues that increased costs and foreign competition will destroy Minnesota's great industry unless the legislature "gives them a break."

Two familiar visitors to capitol corridors are M. J. Galvin and Gordon Forbes — former legislators who represent railroad interests. Two other ex-lawmakers, Lawrence Hall and Ray Quinlivan, speak ably in behalf of the Wine and Spirits Institute and the Minnesota Brewers' Association respectively. Unlike them, the United Temperance Movement of Minnesota wants "to discourage the use of beverage alcohol and other narcotics . . . and . . . promote a higher standard of juvenile and adult conduct, prevent the disastrous effects of intemperance and kindred vices," and so on. While avoiding direct lobbying, the Minnesota Council of Churches alerts its membership to bills affecting social welfare, public morality, and education; and its member groups are quite apt to take pen in hand and relay their demands to their senate and house representatives.

Pleading causes, quoting figures, whitewashing themselves, indicting competitors, keeping government out, getting government in, urging expenditures, urging retrenchments, on they come along with the many other lobbies — a *vox populi* which is not always a *vox Dei*.

And yet it should be reiterated that the lobbies' "right to petition" is undeniable, as is their useful service in keeping hundreds of channels open between the lay person and the professional politician. If the lobbies have become an unofficial house of representatives, this is not necessarily an evil; lobby-less politics might be neater and simpler (though even this is hypothetical) but it would be far less interesting, and, more important, it would be far less representative.

Conflicts of interest

There is an inevitable overlapping between the membership or executive personnel of interest groups and the membership of the legislature. Some lobbies employ a former legislator as their representative, knowing that such a man's personal contacts and political experience will stand them in good stead. A lawyer-legislator may be retained by a particular client not so much because of his professional competence as because of his connections with "sources of power," and he may be paid an unexpectedly handsome fee for minor legal services. There is a great range of inducements — furtive or open, innocent or corrupt — to which legislators are subjected: luncheons, vacation trips, business favors, campaign contributions, and so on.

One can easily see the moral ambiguities here. In defense of the legislator it should be remembered that he is a part-time politician-statesman who is expected to keep his professional or business activities alive during his term of office. Perhaps inevitably he will represent some partial interest or interests which may at times conflict with the general interest, since he is himself elected from a geographical section, supported by a particular faction, and conditioned by his own experiences to a distinct point of view. It is extremely difficult, then, to define the point at which conflicts between special interests and the public interest lead to betrayals of the public trust. Though it can be asserted in a general sense that "no man can serve two masters" the application of this maxim to government is another matter.

In 1957 Governor Freeman appointed a bipartisan Committee on Ethics in Government which was first headed by President Charles J. Turck of Macalester College and later by Rabbi W. Gunther Plaut of St. Paul's Mount Zion Temple. The committee's report in 1958 drew widely from federal and state experiences (particularly in Wisconsin, New York, and California) and addressed itself to a host of related topics involving conflicts of interest, mandatory codes of ethics, campaign tactics, and lobbying. However, legislative implementation of its recommendations has been inconclusive to date. The 1959 session defeated a bill to create a governor's Commission on Ethical Standards together with a code of ethics for legislative as well as administrative personnel. The house overwhelmingly approved a bill (although this did not become law) requiring registration of lobbyists, disclosure of their objectives and activities, and financial accounting — all under criminal penalty for willfully disregarding the requirements or falsifying information. Disliking this approach, the senate adopted a rule (with the Liberals in near-unanimous opposition) requiring a lobbyist merely to register and to disclose to the committee before which he appears whether he "has a pecuniary or other special interest in a measure or proposal different from the public generally." Falsification while not bearing a criminal penalty would bar the offender from again "appearing" before the legislature in any "professional or representative capacity."

There is increasing demand for statutes to regulate legislative influence. Who should be exempted, who is technically a lobbyist and who is not, how frequent and how complete a financial reporting is to be required, who is to enforce what penalties — such are the considerations complicating legislation on the subject. The constitutionally sanctioned right of individuals and groups to speak, to earn a living and to enjoy reasonable financial privacy must be balanced against the right of the public to be represented by men whose ultimate allegiance is given to the total welfare rather than to a small fraction thereof.

Supplementary Materials

MINNESOTA'S DELEGATES TO THE NATION

A COMPLETE list of Minnesota's congressmen may be found in the current *Legislative Manual*. The sketches here are intended to provide some biographical details on the senators who have served the state in the twentieth century and on a few of the more recent representatives from each of the congressional districts.

United States senators

Knute Nelson (1843–1923) was born in Norway but educated in the United States. A Civil War veteran, he moved to Minnesota from Wisconsin in 1871 and operated a farm near Alexandria. His public positions included attorney for Douglas County, state senator, and governor (1893–95). He was a Republican. In the United States Senate from 1895 to 1923 he supported the hard-money position against the inflationary demands of the Populists and Silver Republicans, and along with many other midwestern senators worked for downward revision of tariffs.

Moses Clapp (1851–1929) also moved to the state from Wisconsin. He became a Fergus Falls criminal lawyer and Minnesota attorney general. In 1901 as a regular Republican he was elected over the Silver Republican Charles A. Towne to the Senate vacancy created by the death of Cushman K. Davis. Clapp, known as "the Black Eagle," became the Senate expert on the problems of the Chippewa Indians and on Indian reservations; for a number of years he chaired the Senate Committee on Indian affairs. He also fought for the Hepburn and Elkin acts aimed at regulation of discriminatory rate and rebate practices of the railroads. His Senate incumbency lasted until 1917.

New York-born Frank B. Kellogg (1856–1937) came with his parents to Minnesota at the age of nine. As a St. Paul attorney he became an authority on corporation law. He served on the Interstate Commerce Commission and participated in the Standard Oil and Harriman railroad trust investigations. A Republican, he was elected to the Senate in 1917. As a member of its Foreign Relations Committee, he was one of those who had "mild reservations" about the League of Nations. In 1921–22 he represented the Senate majority party in the Washington arms conferences. Defeated by Henrik Shipstead in 1922, he became United States ambassador to Britain during the Harding administration, in which capacity he took part in the "Dawes plan" negotiations over German war debts. Calvin Coolidge appointed him secretary of state in 1925. He will be remembered for important policy decisions regarding Chinese-American relations and especially for the Kellogg-Briand "outlawry of war" pact signed on August 27, 1928. One year later he received the Nobel peace prize.

Henrik Shipstead (1881–1960), Kellogg's successful Senate opponent, was born in Burbank, Kandiyohi County, practiced dentistry in Glenwood, was that town's mayor from 1911 to 1913, and served as state representative from 1916 to 1921. After breaking off his association with the Republican party, he became the new Farmer-Labor party's first United States senator in 1922. He returned to the Republican fold in 1940. After serving four terms, he was defeated by Edward J. Thye in the 1946 Republican primary.

The highly colorful Magnus Johnson (1871–1936) emigrated from Sweden, worked as a lumberjack in northern Minnesota, Wisconsin, and Michigan, and settled on a 40-acre Meeker County farm in 1893. After terms in the state house of representatives (1915–19) and senate (1919–23) he gravitated toward the Farmer-Labor movement and was a member of the new party's founding committee. He became the Farmer-Laborites' second United States senator by reason of his 1923 victory in a special election for the seat of the deceased Knute Nelson. He was defeated the following year by Republican Thomas D. Schall, by a margin of

8,000 votes out of the 760,000 votes cast. He served one term in the United States House (1933–35), but was defeated in his bid for re-election.

Thomas D. Schall (1876–1935), born near Grand Rapids, Michigan, began his career as a newsboy and circus roustabout. Graduating from Hamline University and the St. Paul College of Law, he practiced law in Minneapolis until he lost his sight in 1907, the victim of a cigar-lighter explosion. He ran unsuccessfully for Congress on the Bull Moose ticket in 1912, but held the 10th District seat in the United States House of Representatives from 1915 to 1925. His close senatorial victory over Magnus Johnson in 1924 provoked charges that he had extorted money from bootleggers by promising them immunity from state or federal prosecution, but he was exonerated by state and senatorial investigating committees. In the Senate he was an implacable critic of the New Deal and of the Olson administration. He died in 1935 after an automobile accident. Governor Olson, who had himself intended to run against Schall in 1936, appointed Elmer Benson to the unexpired term.

Ernest Lundeen (1878–1940), a South Dakotan by birth and a Spanish-American War veteran, graduated from Carleton College and the University of Minnesota Law School. He was a Republican member of the Minnesota house for two terms starting in 1911, and in 1916 he won a seat in the famous War Congress of 1917–19, representing the 5th District. As an opponent of the Wilson administration, of conscription, and of American entry into the war, he was called by Teddy Roosevelt a "microbe" and "a shadow Hun." He became a Farmer-Laborite in the 1920's and represented the 3rd District in Congress from 1933 to 1937. In 1936 he defeated former Governor Theodore Christianson by over 260,000 votes for the Senate, his stand on foreign affairs being an important issue in the campaign. He will be remembered chiefly for his unswerving isolationism but also for his strong support of New Deal social security measures (the Frazier-Lundeen Act). On August 31, 1940, he was killed in an airplane crash.

Joseph H. Ball (1905–   ) was born in Crookston, Minnesota.

An alumnus of Antioch College and the University of Minnesota, he became a reporter on the *Minneapolis Journal* and later on the St. Paul newspapers, where he was an influential and widely read advocate of Stassen Republicanism. Governor Stassen named him to complete Senator Lundeen's term, a post he retained in the next election. A strong internationalist and independent, Ball deserted the Republicans briefly in 1944 to support Roosevelt's fourth term. The conservative labor position he adopted in supporting the Taft-Hartley bill became a salient issue in his 1948 contest with Democrat-Farmer-Laborite Hubert H. Humphrey, who defeated him.

Hubert H. Humphrey (1911–   ) was born in Wallace, South Dakota, graduated from the Denver College of Pharmacy, and was employed as a pharmacist from 1933 to 1937. He received his Bachelor of Arts degree from the University of Minnesota in 1939, his Master of Arts degree from the University of Louisiana in 1940. He served as state director of war production training and re-employment in 1941; state chief of the Minnesota War Service Program in 1942; assistant commissioner of the War Manpower Commission in 1943; instructor in political science at Macalester College, 1943–44; mayor of Minneapolis, 1945–49. When elected to the upper house of Congress in 1948 he was the first DFL senator from the state. He was re-elected in 1954.

Of Norwegian parentage, Edward J. Thye (1896–   ) had been a Dakota County farmer since the early 1920's when he was appointed by Stassen as deputy commissioner of agriculture in 1939. Elected to the lieutenant governorship in 1942, Thye became the state's chief executive after Stassen departed for service in the Navy. In 1944 his popular mandate totaled 61.6 per cent of the vote — the largest margin in any gubernatorial contest to date in the history of the state. Elected to the Senate in 1946 and re-elected in 1952 by a majority of 195,000 votes, Thye became a strong Eisenhower supporter on domestic and foreign policy issues and served on the Agriculture, Small Business, and Appropriations committees. He sponsored the Small Business Act, co-authored Public Law 480 and the Soil Bank plan, and supported the

Farm Home Administration. He was defeated in a third-term attempt by Eugene J. McCarthy in 1958.

Eugene J. McCarthy (1916–   ) was born in Watkins, Minnesota, graduated from St. John's University in Collegeville, Minnesota, and took his M.A. degree at the University of Minnesota in 1939. He taught in public high schools and became a sociology instructor at the College of St. Thomas. He served as chairman of the Ramsey County DFL in 1948, and in November was elected to the United States House of Representatives. There he served on the House committees on Post Office and Civil Service, Agriculture, Interior and Insular Affairs, Banking and Currency, and Ways and Means (this last being the committee on committees for the House Democrats). He represented the Congress in various international meetings: the London Interparliamentary Conference in 1956, the Geneva Trade and Tariffs Conference in 1957, NATO parliamentary conferences in 1956 and 1957, and the World Health Conference in 1958. McCarthy was known for his reflective essays and speeches on political philosophy and for his leadership among liberal Democrats in the House. As Minnesota's junior senator he serves on the influential Senate Finance and Public Works committees.

United States representatives

In the Minnesota delegation elected in 1958 to the House of Representatives, the five Republicans are for the most part strong Eisenhower backers, middle-of-the-roaders on domestic legislation, and advocates of active participation in international affairs. The four Democrat-Farmer-Laborites all belong to the northern and liberal wing of the national Democratic party.

1st District. This agriculturally rich southeastern sector, traditionally the center of Minnesota Republicanism, was for many years served by lawyer-farmer August H. Andresen of Red Wing, who was first elected in 1924 and became the ranking member of the House Agriculture Committee. Before World War II Andresen belonged to that group of midwestern congressmen who were extremely critical of any measures which would compromise

American neutrality by involving this country in international or inter-Allied commitments. Though pro-Eisenhower, Andresen took issue with the president and the secretary of agriculture on a number of specific issues dealing with agriculture and the dairy industry. When he died, Albert H. Quie, who had served in two sessions of the state legislature (1955 and 1957), narrowly won the seat at a special election in February 1958 against DFL contender Eugene Foley. Re-elected in the general election of 1958, Quie serves on the House Agriculture, Education, and Labor committees.

2nd District. Running along the Iowa line, this region was represented from 1921 to 1933 by Republican Frank Clague, a former county attorney, speaker of the Minnesota house, state senator, and district court judge. Clague was one of the candidates for speakership of the United States House in 1931. Elmer J. Ryan was for a number of years the only Minnesota Democrat in Congress; he served from 1935 to 1941. Former McLeod County Attorney Joseph P. O'Hara represented the 2nd District from 1941 until his retirement in 1958. A perennial opponent of "big government," O'Hara objected to heavy expenditures for foreign aid, public power, and nationally administered or initiated welfare programs; he voted against giving the chief executive broad discretion in international commitments. Ancher Nelsen won the seat vacated by O'Hara in 1958. Nelsen had served McLeod County in the state senate continuously from 1935 to 1948, became lieutenant governor in 1952, and accepted an Eisenhower appointment to head the Rural Electrification Administration from 1953 to 1956. He was state Republican chairman from March to June of 1958. Nelsen, who operates a 280-acre diversified farm in McLeod County, has shown particular interest in agricultural problems, in conservation programs, and in low-cost power for farmers. He serves on the House committees on Interstate and Foreign Commerce.

3rd District. The history of this district (which covers northeast Minneapolis, rural Hennepin County, and several counties north and east of Minneapolis) includes the 22-year congressional career of Charles R. Davis, a Republican who joined in the Progressives' fight against the arbitrary rule of Speaker Cannon. His tenure ended in 1925. The 3rd District delegation since his time has included men of varied political backgrounds and viewpoints. Like his predecessor, Ernest Lundeen (1933–37), Henry G. Teigan (1937–39) was prominently involved in early Farmer-Labor activities; he was editor of the Farmer-Labor *Advocate* and later of the *Minnesota Leader*. George MacKinnon, a devoted Stassen supporter in the state house of representatives from 1935 to 1941, represented the district in Congress from 1947 to 1949, during which time he voted in favor of such controversial measures as the Taft-Hartley labor bill, flexible price supports, and the Mundt-Nixon internal security bill. In the 1952 campaign MacKinnon acted as consultant to Nixon and in 1958, after service as United States district attorney in Minnesota, he became the GOP candidate in the gubernatorial race against Freeman. Roy W. Wier defeated MacKinnon in 1948 and has enjoyed continuous re-election ever since, though often by narrow margins. Before election to the congressional post, he served on the Minneapolis Board of Education (1939–49); he had been for twenty-five years the financial secretary and organizer of the Minneapolis Central Labor Union; and as state representative he had been a pro-Olson member of the Liberal caucus in the Minnesota legislature (1933–39). A member of the House's Education, Labor, and District of Columbia committees, he supported the Truman-Fair Deal program, especially in such hotly contested areas as public power, tax benefits for lower income groups, rights of labor unions, loyalty and security programs, and public housing.

4th District. Except for one term in the mid-thirties, St. Paul–Ramsey County was represented by Melvin J. Maas (Rep.) continuously from 1927 to 1945. Rather conservative on domestic issues, Maas was prominent in military and defense affairs, chaired the House Naval Affairs Committee, and alone among Minnesota congressmen voted for the fortification of Guam in 1939. A former marine combat officer, now blind, Major General Maas is presently chairman of the President's Committee on Employment of the Physically Handicapped. Succeeding him were Frank T. Starkey (DFL; 1945–47), long-time St. Paul labor leader and now state commissioner of employment and security; Edward J. Devitt (Rep.; 1947–49), now United States district judge; and Eugene J. McCarthy (DFL; 1949–59), now United States senator. Joseph E. Karth (DFL) defeated Republican Frank S. Farrell by over 16,000 votes for the seat vacated by McCarthy. A World War II combat veteran, a union official, and a four-term member of the Minnesota house (1951–59) and chairman of its Labor Committee, Karth serves on the Committee on Science and Astronautics of the United States House of Representatives.

5th District. This district, which now includes much of south and west Minneapolis, has in recent decades sent a number of distinguished men to the House of Representatives. The list includes Walter H. Newton (Rep.; 1919–29), future secretary to President Hoover; W. I. Nolan (Rep.; 1929–33), a speaker of the Minnesota house and Minnesota's lieutenant governor from 1925 to 1929; Theodore Christianson (Rep.; 1935–37), three-term governor of Minnesota; and Dr. Walter H. Judd (Rep.), the incumbent since 1943. A native of Nebraska and a World War I veteran, Judd served for a number of years in South China as a medical missionary under the Foreign Mission Board of the Congregational church. As a highly influential member of the House Foreign Affairs Committee he has become nationally known as a strong supporter of Chiang Kai-shek and the Nationalist China regime on Formosa. Among the many bills authored or sponsored by Judd are those dealing with United States membership in the United Nations and such related organizations as World Health, the International Children's Emergency Fund, and Technical Aid. He supports NATO and SEATO and is a key Eisenhower supporter on domestic issues, opposing measures tending to lead to heavily increased spending for public works, public housing, and public power. He was a delegate to the UN General Assembly in 1957 and to the World Health assemblies in 1950 and 1958.

6th District. This district is the geographical center of Minnesota — an area that includes Stearns County and St. Cloud and shows a heavy concentration of voters of German descent. It was once represented by Charles A. Lindbergh (Rep.; 1907–17), who voted against United States entry into World War I and the Payne-Aldrich tariff, supported the Pujo investigations of the money trusts, and sided with the bloc of Republican insurgents and reformers. His congressional attacks on war profiteers and war propaganda furnished his opponents with lively campaign issues when he vied unsuccessfully with Burnquist for the gubernatorial nomination in the 1918 Republican primary. Harold Knutson, the Republican farmer-newspaper editor who represented the district from 1917 to 1933 and again from 1935 to 1949, rose to the chairmanship of the powerful House Ways and Means Committee. As one of the stalwarts of midwestern isolationism in the pre-Pearl Harbor era he opposed vigorously the New Deal, both in domestic and foreign policy. Fred Marshall (DFL) of Grove City, who defeated Knutson in a close election in 1948, has since been the most direct and personal spokesman for agricultural interests among the DFL congressmen. Besides operating a fourth-generation family farm, Marshall served in the state Agricultural Adjustment Administration from 1937 to 1941 and held the office of state farm security administrator for seven years. He is the ranking majority member of the House Agriculture Committee's subcommittee on Department of Agriculture appropriations and a member of the House Appropriations Committee.

7th District. This southwestern area along the South Dakota line sent to Washington the famous Andrew J. Volstead (Rep.; 1903–23), the "father of prohibition." Volstead was a St. Olaf graduate, city attorney and mayor of Granite Falls, and Yellow Medicine's county attorney; in the House he became chairman of the Judiciary Committee and was an important legislative figure in matters of federal law enforcement. O. J. Kvale (1923–29), a Lutheran minister and one of the few Farmer-Labor congressmen, defeated Volstead and served as a spokesman for agricultural discontent until his accidental death. His son, Paul John Kvale, also a Farmer-Laborite, succeeded him but was defeated by H. Carl

Andersen in 1938. A Republican and a Tyler, Minnesota, farmer, Andersen has given strong support to soil and water conservation programs. Recently he has shown much interest in increased federal appropriations for cancer and heart research. On domestic issues Andersen generally sides with those midwestern Republicans who criticize the extension of international commitments and who resist New Deal and Fair Deal legislative objectives. In the 80th and 83rd Congresses Andersen chaired the subcommittee for agriculture of the House Committee on Appropriations, of which he is now ranking minority member; he also belongs to the subcommittee for public works and atomic energy.

8th District. Including Duluth, St. Louis County, and the iron-mining country, the 8th District is now a DFL stronghold, but it was earlier represented for fourteen years by Republican William A. Pittenger (1929–33, 1935–37, 1939–47). Pittenger graduated from Wabash College and the Harvard Law School, served in the state legislature (1917–19), and while in Congress made his influence felt in the Rivers and Harbors Committee, where he was an advocate of the St. Lawrence Seaway. He voted for the lend-lease agreements on the eve of World War II and for extension of the draft in 1941. Certain New Deal measures, as for example WPA and NYA, met with his approval. John A. Blatnik defeated Pittenger in 1946 and has been re-elected with huge majorities ever since, his 70,000 plurality of 1956 standing as the most decisive victory in the history of the state's congressional elections. After graduating from Winona State Teachers College, Blatnik did postgraduate work in public administration at the universities of Chicago and Minnesota, taught school, and served in the state senate (1941), where he was instrumental in the passage of the Minnesota Taconite Tax Law. During World War II he served in Air Corps Intelligence and in the O.S.S. and was a paratroop officer working behind enemy lines in northern Yugoslavia. As the dean of the DFL congressional delegation his major interests are natural resources, social welfare legislation, the St. Lawrence Seaway, federal water-pollution control, refugee and immigration measures, foreign aid, and support of the UN and its technical assistance programs. He is a member of the House committees on Public Works (chairman of the subcommittee on rivers and harbors) and Government Operations.

9th District. Encompassing Minnesota's sparsely populated northwest corner, this district for many years ran second only to the 7th District in its allegiance to the Farmer-Laborites. Farmer-Labor stalwart Knud Wefald represented the district from 1923 to 1927 and Richard Thompson Buckler from 1935 to 1943. Buckler, who had been the state senator from Polk County for twelve years, considered himself a follower of the true Progressive tradition. In Congress he fought for farm cooperatives, for lower interest rates for farmers, for federal old-age pensions, and for governmental ownership and control of a central banking system. His successor, Harold C. Hagen (1943–55), once a Farmer-Laborite, later a Republican, had been a social studies teacher, an athletic coach, a newspaper publisher, and for eight years Buckler's congressional secretary. Besides speaking for agricultural interests Hagen showed much interest in the problems of postal employees and civil servants. In 1954 he was defeated by Mrs. Coya Knutson, a former music teacher and a two-term member of the Minnesota legislature (1951 and 1953). In Congress she became the first woman member of the House Agricultural Committee and was identified with those new Democrats from the Midwest who opposed the Eisenhower position on agriculture, public power, credit, and taxation. During Mrs. Knutson's re-election bid in 1958 her husband's alleged objections to her political career grew into a nationally publicized "Coya Come Home" incident. Although the winner over Marvin E. Evenson in the DFL primary, she lost in the general election to Republican Odin Langen in a contest decided by slightly over 1,300 votes. Langen, a former state representative (1951–59) and the minority leader in the Minnesota house in the 1957 session, serves on the House Committee on Interior and Insular Affairs.

GOVERNORS OF THE STATE

Name and Party	Term in Office
Territorial	
Alexander Ramsey	1849–1853
Willis A. Gorman	1853–1857
Samuel Medary	1857–1858
State	
Henry H. Sibley (Democrat)	1858–1860
Alexander Ramsey (Republican)	1860–1863
Henry A. Swift (Republican)	1863–1864
Stephen Miller (Republican)	1864–1866
William R. Marshall (Republican)	1866–1870
Horace Austin (Republican)	1870–1874
Cushman K. Davis (Republican)	1874–1876
John S. Pillsbury (Republican)	1876–1882
Lucius F. Hubbard (Republican)	1882–1887
Andrew R. McGill (Republican)	1887–1889
William R. Merriam (Republican)	1889–1893
Knute Nelson (Republican)	1893–1895
David M. Clough (Republican)	1895–1899
John Lind (Democrat)	1899–1901
Samuel R. Van Sant (Republican)	1901–1905
John A. Johnson (Democrat)	1905–1909
Adolph O. Eberhart (Republican)	1909–1915
Winfield S. Hammond (Democrat)	1915
Joseph A. A. Burnquist (Republican)	1915–1921
J. A. O. Preus (Republican)	1921–1925
Theodore Christianson (Republican)	1925–1931
Floyd B. Olson (Farmer-Labor)	1931–1936
Hjalmar Petersen (Farmer-Labor)	1936–1937
Elmer A. Benson (Farmer-Labor)	1937–1939
Harold E. Stassen (Republican)	1939–1943
Edward J. Thye (Republican)	1943–1947
Luther W. Youngdahl (Republican)	1947–1951
C. Elmer Anderson (Republican)	1951–1955
Orville L. Freeman (Democrat-Farmer-Laborite)	1955–

VOTING STATISTICS

Table I. Major Party Vote for President in
Minnesota, 1920–1956 *

Year	Candidate and Party	Votes Cast	Percentage of Total
1920	*Warren G. Harding* (Rep.)	519,421	70.6
	James M. Cox (Dem.)	142,994	19.4
	Eugene V. Debs (Soc.)	56,106	7.6
1924	*Calvin Coolidge* (Rep.)	420,759	51.2
	John W. Davis (Dem.)	55,913	6.8
	Robert M. LaFollette (Ind.)	339,192	41.3
1928	*Herbert Hoover* (Rep.)	560,977	57.8
	Alfred E. Smith (Dem.)	396,451	40.8
1932	*Franklin D. Roosevelt* (Dem.)	600,806	59.9
	Herbert Hoover (Rep.)	363,959	36.3
1936	*Franklin D. Roosevelt* (Dem.)	698,811	61.8
	Alfred M. Landon (Rep.)	350,461	31.0
1940	*Franklin D. Roosevelt* (Dem.)	644,196	51.5
	Wendell L. Willkie (Rep.)	596,274	47.7
1944	*Franklin D. Roosevelt* (Dem.)	589,864	52.4
	Thomas E. Dewey (Rep.)	527,416	46.9
1948	*Harry S. Truman* (Dem.)	692,966	57.2
	Thomas E. Dewey (Rep.)	483,617	39.9
1952	*Dwight D. Eisenhower* (Rep.)	763,211	55.3
	Adlai E. Stevenson (Dem.)	608,458	44.1
1956	*Dwight D. Eisenhower* (Rep.)	719,302	53.7
	Adlai E. Stevenson (Dem.)	617,525	46.1

* Votes for candidates of the Industrial Government party, Communist party, Socialist Worker party, and other minor political groups were omitted because of their small number of votes; hence the figures do not total 100 per cent.

117

Table II. Major Party Vote for Senator in Minnesota, 1916–1958*

Year	Candidate and Party	Votes Cast	Percentage of Total
1916	*Frank B. Kellogg* (Rep.)	185,159	48.6
	Daniel W. Lawler (Dem.)	117,541	30.8
	W. G. Calderwood (Prohib.)	78,425	20.6
1918	*Knute Nelson* (Rep.)	206,684	60.1
	W. G. Calderwood (Prohib.)	137,296	39.9
1922	*Henrik Shipstead* (FL)	325,372	47.1
	Frank B. Kellogg (Rep.)	241,833	35.0
	A. Olesen (Dem.)	123,624	17.9
1924	*Thomas D. Schall* (Rep.)	388,594	46.5
	Magnus Johnson (FL)	380,646	45.5
	John J. Farrell (Dem.)	53,709	6.4
1928	*Henrik Shipstead* (FL)	665,169	65.4
	Arthur E. Nelson (Rep.)	342,992	33.7
1930	*Thomas D. Schall* (Rep.)	293,626	37.6
	Ernest Lundeen (FL)	178,671	22.9
	Einar Hoidale (Dem.)	282,018	36.1
	Charles Lund (Ind. by Pet.)	20,669	2.6
1934	*Henrik Shipstead* (FL)	503,379	49.9
	H. J. Holmberg (Rep.)	200,083	19.8
	Einar Hoidale (Dem.)	294,757	29.2
1936	*Ernest Lundeen* (FL)	663,363	62.2
	Theodore Christianson (Rep.)	402,404	37.8
1940	*Henrik Shipstead* (Rep.)	641,049	53.0
	Elmer A. Benson (FL)	310,875	25.7
	John E. Regan (Dem.)	248,658	20.6
1942	*Joseph H. Ball* (Rep.)	356,297	47.0
	Elmer A. Benson (FL)	213,965	28.2
	Ed Murphy (Dem.)	78,959	10.4
	Martin A. Nelson (Ind. Prog.)	109,226	14.4
1946	*Edward J. Thye* (Rep.)	517,775	58.9
	Theodore Jorgenson (DFL)	349,520	39.8
1948	*Hubert H. Humphrey* (DFL)	729,494	59.8
	Joseph H. Ball (Rep.)	485,801	39.8
1952	*Edward J. Thye* (Rep.)	785,649	56.6
	William Carlson (DFL)	590,011	42.5
1954	*Hubert H. Humphrey* (DFL)	642,193	56.4
	Val Bjornson (Rep.)	479,619	42.1
1958	*Eugene J. McCarthy* (DFL)	608,847	52.9
	Edward J. Thye (Rep.)	535,629	46.6

* Votes for candidates of the Industrial Government party, Communist party, Socialist Worker party, and other minor political groups were omitted because of their small number of votes; hence the figures do not total 100 per cent.

Table III. Major Party Vote for Governor in Minnesota, 1920–1958*

Year	Candidate and Party	Votes Cast	Percentage of Total
1920	*J. A. O. Preus* (Rep.)	415,805	53.1
	Henrik Shipstead (FL)	281,402	35.9
	L. C. Hodgson (Dem.)	81,293	10.4
1922	*J. A. O. Preus* (Rep.)	309,756	45.2
	Magnus Johnson (FL)	295,479	43.1
	Edward Indrehus (Dem.)	79,903	11.6
1924	*Theodore Christianson* (Rep.)	406,692	48.7
	Floyd B. Olson (FL)	366,029	43.8
	Carlos Avery (Dem.)	49,353	5.9
1926	*Theodore Christianson* (Rep.)	395,779	56.5
	Magnus Johnson (FL)	266,845	38.1
	Alfred Jaques (Dem.)	38,008	5.4
1928	*Theodore Chistianson* (Rep.)	549,857	55.0
	Ernest Lundeen (FL)	227,193	22.7
	Andrew Nelson (Dem.)	213,734	21.4
1930	*Floyd B. Olson* (FL)	473,154	59.3
	Ray P. Chase (Rep.)	289,528	36.3
1932	*Floyd B. Olson* (FL)	522,438	50.6
	Earle Brown (Rep.)	334,081	32.3
	John E. Regan (Dem.)	169,859	16.4
1934	*Floyd B. Olson* (FL)	468,812	44.6
	Martin A. Nelson (Rep.)	396,359	37.7
	John E. Regan (Dem.)	176,928	16.8
1936	*Elmer A. Benson* (FL)	680,342	60.7
	Martin A. Nelson (Rep.)	431,841	38.6
1938	*Harold E. Stassen* (Rep.)	678,839	59.9
	Elmer A. Benson (FL)	387,263	34.2
	Thomas Gallagher (Dem.)	65,875	5.8
1940	*Harold E. Stassen* (Rep.)	654,686	52.1
	Hjalmar Petersen (FL)	459,609	36.5
	Ed Murphy (Dem.)	140,021	11.1
1942	*Harold E. Stassen* (Rep.)	409,800	51.6
	Hjalmar Petersen (FL)	299,917	37.8
	John D. Sullivan (Dem.)	75,151	9.5
1944	*Edward J. Thye* (Rep.)	701,185	61.6
	Byron G. Allen (DFL)	430,132	37.8
1946	*Luther W. Youngdahl* (Rep.)	519,067	59.0
	Harold H. Barker (DFL)	349,565	39.7

*Votes for candidates of the Industrial Government party, Communist party, Socialist Worker party, and other minor political groups were omitted because of their small number of votes; hence the figures do not total 100 per cent.

119

Table III — Continued

Year	Candidate and Party	Votes Cast	Percentage of Total
1948	*Luther W. Youngdahl* (Rep.)	643,572	53.1
	Charles L. Halsted (DFL)	545,766	45.1
1950	*Luther W. Youngdahl* (Rep.)	635,800	60.7
	Harry H. Peterson (DFL)	400,637	38.3
1952	*C. Elmer Anderson* (Rep.)	785,125	55.3
	Orville L. Freeman (DFL)	624,480	44.0
1954	*Orville L. Freeman* (DFL)	607,099	52.7
	C. Elmer Anderson (Rep.)	538,865	46.8
1956	*Orville L. Freeman* (DFL)	731,180	51.4
	Ancher Nelsen (Rep.)	685,196	48.2
1958	*Orville L. Freeman* (DFL)	658,326	56.8
	George MacKinnon (Rep.)	490,731	42.3

Table IV. Comparison of Vote Cast for DFL Candidate for Governor in 1956 and 1958 and for Republican Candidate for President in 1956 in Each County (Identified by Total Population and Percentage of Urban Population)

County	1950 Population	Percentage of Urban Population	Percentage of Vote Received by Freeman		Percentage of Vote Received by Eisenhower (in 1956)
			1956	1958	
Aitkin	14,327	..*	52	58	45
Anoka	35,579	54	61	61	41
Becker	24,836	23	56	57	45
Beltrami	24,962	40	55	58	46
Benton	15,911	40	45	54	53
Big Stone	9,607	27	61	66	40
Blue Earth	38,327	49	38	44	63
Brown	25,895	59	32	39	65
Carlton	24,584	31	67	71	36
Carver	18,155	..	31	37	66
Cass	19,468	..	46	53	53
Chippewa	16,739	36	53	56	46
Chisago	12,669	..	48	55	50
Clay	30,363	49	54	59	48
Clearwater	10,204	..	64	68	36
Cook	2,900	..	49	51	57
Cottonwood	15,763	20	37	42	60
Crow Wing	30,875	50	49	56	48
Dakota	49,019	64	53	58	47
Dodge	12,624	..	41	44	57
Douglas	21,304	30	49	54	50
Faribault	23,879	16	39	45	60
Fillmore	24,465	..	37	44	61
Freeborn	34,517	39	53	58	47
Goodhue	32,118	33	40	47	59
Grant	9,542	..	53	55	45
Hennepin	676,579	91	49	55	52
Houston	14,435	..	38	45	60
Hubbard	11,085	27	41	48	56
Isanti	12,123	25	57	61	43
Itasca	33,321	18	64	67	38
Jackson	16,306	20	54	55	48
Kanabec	9,192	..	51	56	48
Kandiyohi	28,644	33	60	65	40
Kittson	9,649	..	67	69	37
Koochiching	16,910	37	66	73	37
Lac qui Parle	14,545	..	51	56	48
Lake	7,781	57	67	72	37
Lake of the Woods	4,955	..	64	68	38
Le Sueur	19,088	14	45	51	52
Lincoln	10,150	..	56	57	43
Lyon	22,253	40	49	55	50

Source: Unpublished data, collected under the supervision of Ivan Kubanis, Department of Political Science, University of Minnesota, 1959.

* Percentages are not given for counties with less than 2,500 urban population.

Table IV — Continued

County	1950 Population	Percentage of Urban Population	Percentage of Vote Received by Freeman		Percentage of Vote Received by Eisenhower (in 1956)
			1956	1958	
McLeod	22,198	34	35	43	62
Mahnomen	7,059	..	68	68	32
Marshall	16,125	..	64	68	37
Martin	25,655	32	35	39	66
Meeker	18,966	24	46	54	53
Mille Lacs	15,165	..	49	56	50
Morrison	25,832	26	51	56	46
Mower	42,277	55	55	60	48
Murray	14,801	..	51	52	49
Nicollet	20,929	60	38	47	61
Nobles	22,435	35	51	56	50
Norman	12,909	..	61	66	42
Olmsted	48,228	62	41	47	62
Otter Tail	51,320	25	37	39	61
Pennington	12,965	53	62	68	41
Pine	18,223	..	58	61	42
Pipestone	14,003	38	45	47	54
Polk	35,900	35	60	65	42
Pope	12,862	21	52	56	47
Ramsey	355,332	95	56	60	46
Red Lake	6,806	..	70	72	30
Redwood	22,127	17	36	40	61
Renville	23,954	..	44	51	52
Rice	36,235	65	38	46	59
Rock	11,278	32	37	36	60
Roseau	14,505	..	65	67	34
St. Louis	206,062	75	66	68	37
Scott	16,486	19	51	59	49
Sherburne	10,661	25	45	51	55
Sibley	15,816	..	34	38	62
Stearns	70,681	37	42	50	58
Steele	21,155	48	38	45	61
Stevens	11,106	34	45	51	53
Swift	15,837	22	62	66	37
Todd	25,420	11	46	49	50
Traverse	8,053	..	62	64	41
Wabasha	16,878	21	39	47	59
Wadena	12,806	31	41	46	59
Waseca	14,957	33	36	42	60
Washington	34,544	41	45	50	52
Watonwan	13,881	28	36	45	62
Wilkin	10,567	34	49	55	50
Winona	39,841	63	43	51	55
Wright	27,716	..	44	50	54
Yellow Medicine	16,279	12	52	57	46

Table V. Proposed Amendments to the Minnesota Constitution, 1948–1958

No.	Year on Ballot	Provision of Minnesota Constitution to Be Amended	Purpose of Amendment	Adopted or Rejected	Yes Vote	No Vote	Total Vote at General Election	Percentage Yes Is of Total
1	1948	Art. IX, Sect. 5	To provide for a 50-50 apportionment of excise tax on petroleum products	R	534,538	539,224	1,257,804	42.50
2	1948	Art. XIV, Sect. 1	To authorize submission of two or more amendments without requiring voters to vote separately on each amendment	R	319,667	621,523	1,257,804	25.41
3	1948	Art. XIV, Sect. 2	To authorize ⅔ of the legislature to call for a constitutional convention without submitting the question to the voters	R	294,842	641,013	1,257,804	23.44
4	1948	Add a new article	To authorize the state to pay a veterans' bonus	A	664,703	420,518	1,257,804	52.85
5	1950	Art. IX, Sect. 1	To authorize diversion of 1% of the proceeds of the occupation mining tax to the Veterans' Compensation Fund	A	594,092	290,870	1,067,967	55.63
6	1950	Art. IV, Sect. 32 (b) be repealed and VIII, 2, be amended	To authorize Forestry Management Funds by diverting certain proceeds (25%) from Public Land Trust Fund	R	367,013	465,239	1,067,967	34.37
7	1950	Art. IX, Sect. 5	To provide for a 50%-44%-6% apportionment of the excise tax on petroleum products proceeds	R	420,530	456,346	1,067,967	39.38

Table V — Continued

No.	Year on Ballot	Provision of Minnesota Constitution to Be Amended	Purpose of Amendment	Adopted or Rejected	Yes Vote	No Vote	Total Vote at General Election	Percentage Yes Is of Total
8........	1952	Art. VIII, Sect. 6	To authorize a change in the investment and loan requirements governing permanent school and university funds	R	604,384	500,490	1,460,326	41.39
9........	1952	Art. XIV, adding a new Sect. 3	To provide for a 60% popular majority of voters voting on the question before a new state constitution can be considered legally ratified by the electorate	R	656,618	424,492	1,460,326	44.96
10........	1952	Art. VII, Sect. 1	To clarify who shall be entitled to vote	R	716,670	371,508	1,460,326	49.08
11........	1952	Art. VI, Sect. 7	To permit the legislature to extend probate court jurisdiction by a ⅔ vote	R	646,608	443,005	1,460,326	44.28
12........	1952	Art. XVI, Sect. 3	To provide for a 65%-10%-25% apportionment of the excise tax on motor vehicles proceeds	R	580,316	704,336	1,460,326	39.74
13........	1954	Art. VI, Sect. 7	To permit the legislature to define qualifications and to extend jurisdiction of probate judges by a ⅔ vote	A	610,138	308,888	1,168,101	52.23
14........	1954	Art. X, Sect. 3	To empower the legislature to limit the liability of stockholders of state banks	A	624,611	290,039	1,168,101	53.47

Table V — Continued

No.	Year on Ballot	Provision of Minnesota Constitution to Be Amended	Purpose of Amendment	Adopted or Rejected	Yes Vote	No Vote	Total Vote at General Election	Percentage Yes Is of Total
15	1954	Art. XIV, Sect. 3 (new); Art. IX, Sect. 4 (not to apply)	To provide for a 60% popular vote before a new state constitution can be held ratified and to remove the constitutional bar against members of the legislature serving in a constitutional convention	A	638,818	266,434	1,168,101	54.69
16	1954	Art. V, Sect. 4	To permit gubernatorial appointments in case of vacancy in certain offices to run until the end of the term or Jan. 1 and so eliminate the need for election to short terms (Nov. to Jan.)	A	636,237	282,212	1,168,101	54.47
17	1956	Art. VI	To permit the legislature to recognize the judicial power of the state	A	939,957	307,178	1,443,856	65.10
18	1956	New Art. XVI in place of Art. XVI and Art. IX, Sect. 16	To authorize the consolidation of present trunk highway articles and sections, to increase state aid and supervision of public highways, to permit tax of motor vehicles and fuel, and to apportion moneys for highway purposes on the basis of 62%-29%-9% to state and local government highways	A	1,060,063	230,707	1,443,856	73.42

Table V — Continued

No.	Year on Ballot	Provision of Minnesota Constitution to Be Amended	Purpose of Amendment	Adopted or Rejected	Yes Vote	No Vote	Total Vote at General Election	Percentage Yes Is of Total
19	1956	Art. IX, Sect. 1A	To authorize the legislature to divert 50% of occupation mining tax proceeds earmarked for education from permanent trust funds to current educational needs	A	1,084,627	209,311	1,443,856	75.12
20	1958	Art. XI and IV, Sect. 33, and repealing Art. IV, Sect. 36	To authorize the legislature to revise and consolidate provisions on local government, home rule, and special laws	A	712,552	309,848	1,178,173	60.48
21	1958	Art. V, Sect. 3, and Sect. 5	To provide for 4-year terms for state constitutional officers to take effect for terms beginning in 1963	A	641,887	382,505	1,178,173	54.48
22	1958	Art. IV, Sect. 9	To permit members of the legislature to hold certain elective and nonelective state offices	R	576,300	430,112	1,178,173	48.91

Source: G. Theodore Mitau, "Constitutional Change by Amendment: Recommendations of the Minnesota Constitutional Commission in Ten Years' Perspective," *Minnesota Law Review*, 44:461 (1960).

Bibliographical Note and Index

A NOTE ON SOURCES AND FURTHER READINGS

For more extensive bibliographical suggestions, see G. Theodore Mitau, *Selected Bibliography of Research in Minnesota Government, Politics, and Public Finance* (St. Paul, 1960; distributed by the Minnesota Historical Society). The *Legislative Manual* (published biennially by the Minnesota secretary of state), often referred to as the "Blue Book," is a source of much pertinent data on state government and elections.

Chapter I. Party Patterns, Issues, and Leaders

The classic treatise on Minnesota history up to the end of World War I is William Watts Folwell, *A History of Minnesota* (4 vols.; St. Paul: Minnesota Historical Society, 1921–30); a much briefer but thoroughly competent survey of Minnesota history to the early 1930's can be found in Theodore C. Blegen, *Building Minnesota* (New York: D. C. Heath and Co., 1938). An authoritative analysis of the development of the Minnesota constitution is presented in William Anderson and Albert J. Lobb, *A History of the Constitution of Minnesota* (Minneapolis: University of Minnesota, 1921). On some recent changes, see G. Theodore Mitau, "Constitutional Change by Amendment: Recommendations of the Minnesota Constitutional Commission in Ten Years' Perspective," *Minnesota Law Review*, 44:461 (1960).

Midwest protest movements and the story of the Nonpartisan League are thoroughly examined in John D. Hicks, *The Populist Revolt* (Minneapolis: University of Minnesota Press, 1931); Theodore Saloutos and John D. Hicks, *Agricultural Discontent in the Middle West, 1900–1939* (Madison: University of Wisconsin Press, 1951); and Robert L. Morlan, *Political Prairie Fire: The Nonpartisan League, 1915–1922* (Minneapolis: University of Minnesota Press, 1955). Two unpublished Ph.D. theses, prepared at the University of Minnesota, provide analyses of the Farmer-Labor party and Stassen Republicanism: Arthur Naftalin, "The Farmer Labor Party in Minnesota" (1945); and Ivan Hinderaker, "Harold Stassen and Developments in the Republican Party in Minnesota, 1937–1943" (1949). On one aspect of DFL history, see G. Theodore Mitau, "The Democratic-Farmer-Labor Party Schism of 1948," *Minnesota History*, 34-187–94 (Spring 1955). The platforms of Minnesota political parties (1849–1938) were graciously made available to me by Theodore C. Blegen from his collection.

There are some excellent works on Minnesota governors: George M. Stephenson, *John Lind of Minnesota* (Minneapolis: University of Minnesota Press, 1935); George H. Mayer, *The Political Career of Floyd B. Olson* (Minneapolis: University Press, 1951); Winifred G. Helmes, *John A. Johnson: The People's Governor* (Minneapolis: University of Minnesota Press, 1949); Robert Esbjornson, *A Christian in Politics: Luther W. Youngdahl* (Minneapolis: T. S. Denison Co., 1955).

Harold E. Stassen has outlined his own position in *Where I Stand* (Garden City, N.Y.: Doubleday and Co., 1947). Articles on nineteenth-century protest leaders have appeared in *Minnesota History*: Donald F. Warner, "Prelude to Populism," 32:129–46 (September 1951); Carl H. Chrislock, "Sidney M. Owen, An Editor in Politics," 36:109–26 (December 1958); Martin Ridge, "Ignatius Donnelly, Minnesota Congressman, 1863–69," 36:173–83 (March 1959). The presidential prospects of Hubert H. Humphrey are discussed in Walter T. Ridder, "Hustling Hubert Makes His Bid," *Saturday Evening Post*, 231:38–39, 94–98 (April 1959). A campaign biography is Michael Amrine's *This Is Humphrey: The Story of a Senator* (New York: Doubleday and Co., 1960).

Chapter 2. Election Law and Party Organization

An excellent detailed description of various aspects of Minnesota election law and administration is found in "Election Laws" (mimeographed; Minneapolis: Minnesota League of Women Voters, March 1958). Some details on local election dates and procedures are given in Floyd O. Flom and Luther J. Pickrel, *In a Democracy Politics Is Your Job*, Public Affairs Series, University of Minnesota Agricultural Extension Service Pamphlet 201 (1958). On the direct primary, see Clarence C. Hein, "The Operation of the Direct Primary in Minnesota: Nominations for State-Wide and Congressional Office" (Unpublished Ph.D. thesis, University of Minnesota, 1956). On the legal status of political parties, see G. Theodore Mitau, "The Status of Political Party Organization in Minnesota Law," *Minnesota Law Review*, 40:561–79 (April 1956). On various aspects of campaign financing, see Elston E. Roady, "Florida's New Campaign Expense Laws and the Democratic Gubernatorial Primaries," *American Political Science Review*, 48:-465–76 (June 1954); G. Theodore Mitau, "Selected Aspects of Centralized and Decentralized Control over Campaign Finance: A Commentary on S 636," *University of Chicago Law Review*, 23:620–29 (Summer 1956); John C. Obert, "Money, Politics and the Minnesota Story," *Nieman Reports* (Cambridge, Mass.: Harvard University, October 1957). The latter gives the account of the Alexandria experiment.

Chapter 3. A Partisan Nonpartisan Legislature

On the nonpartisanship issue, see Charles R. Adrian, "The Origins of Minnesota's Non-Partisan Legislature," *Minnesota History*, 33:155–64 (Winter 1952), and "The Non-Partisan Legislature in Minnesota" (Unpublished Ph.D. thesis, University of Minnesota, 1950); Ralph S. Fjelstad, "How about Party Labels?" *National Municipal Review*, 44:359–64 (July 1955); Arthur Naftalin, "The Failure of the Farmer-Labor Party to Capture Control of the Minnesota Legislature," *American Political Science Review*, 38:71–78 (February 1944).

The data on state legislators are taken in part from William P. Tucker, "Characteristics of State Legislators," *Social Science*, 30:94–98 (April 1955), and in part from a series of articles by Wallace Mitchell which ran in the *Minneapolis Star* from November 26, 1958, through January 6, 1959.

Chapter 4. Lobbies before the Legislature

I should like to acknowledge gratefully the aid given me in connection with this chapter by Prof. Floyd O. Flom of the University of Minnesota, who made available a number of interview case studies prepared by students in his course on state government.

BIBLIOGRAPHICAL NOTE

The best treatment to date of the role of lobbies and special interests in the Minnesota government is a series of six articles, "Ethics in Government," by John C. McDonald, published in the *Minneapolis Tribune*, March 24–29, 1958.

Various publications of interest groups themselves provided statements of aims and data. League of Women Voters: *Facts about the League of Women Voters* (Washington, D.C.: League of Women Voters of the United States, 1958). Minnesota Employers' Association: *Minnesota Legislature, 61st Session 1959* (St. Paul: Minnesota Employers' Association, 1959); *Guide Post* (St. Paul), issues of January 19 and July 17, 1959. Labor groups: among the most comprehensive of the legislative reports issued by the various groups are "Biennial Reports" published by the Railroad Brotherhoods Legislative Board, and "Legislative Report" published by the Minnesota AFL-CIO Federation of Labor; see also George W. Lawson, *History of Labor in Minnesota* (St. Paul: Minnesota State Federation of Labor, 1955). Farm groups: *Farm Bureau Policies for 1959* (Boston: American Farm Bureau Federation, December 1958); "Agricultural Policies," Resolutions Adopted by the House of Delegates of the Minnesota Farm Bureau Federation at the Fortieth Annual Meeting, St. Paul, November 17, 18, 19, 1958; "Minnesota Farmers Union State Program and Policies for 1959," Adopted at the 17th Annual Convention, November 24–25, 1958. Minnesota Education Association: "1959 Legislative Objectives" (St. Paul: Minnesota Education Association, 1959); "Report of Legislative Committee," *Minnesota Journal of Education*, 39:1–64 (September 1958).

The report of the Governor's Committee on Ethics in Government was issued in St. Paul in January 1959.

INDEX

132